OTHERNESS

Adventures and Mishaps of an Unprepared Traveller

Maggie Kate Harris

Published in Australia in 2016 by Maggie Harris
Carrara Qld 4211

National Library of Australia Cataloguing-in-Publication entry:

Author:	Harris, Maggie
Title:	Otherness: adventures and mishaps of an
	unprepared traveller / Maggie Harris
ISBN:	9781533651037 (paperback)
Subjects:	Harris, Maggie – Travel.
	Travelers' writings, Australian.
	Self-actualization (Psychology) in women.
Dewey No:	910.4

Dedication

'Sallah! I said no camels, that's five camels! Can't you count?!'
– Indiana Jones and the Last Crusade

To all of the story tellers who taught me to dream
of adventure.

And to my dad, with whom I always had a soft place
to land.

Acknowledgements

Thank you to the people I've met along the way. Without the camaraderie of fellow travellers, I may not be here to tell tales of my small adventures. Always at hand to lend a shoulder, a lift, Band-Aid, a restaurant recommendation, a can of hairspray and even a rescue; I hope I've paid it forward.

To Dad, thank you for your scolding, your encouragement, and in your later years, your softness. Everybody needs a hero. You were mine.

Jacqui, thank you for your love and support and phenomenal cooking. Thank you for being you; for loving my dad, for calling me 'daughter' and for always believing in me. Most of all, thank you for having a sense of humour about the insane situations I sometimes find myself in.

Julie, for casting the first critical (and very kind) eye over this book. For encouraging me to make it happen. You don't know just how much it meant.

Finally, my husband Joel. Thank you for picking up the pieces when it all falls apart and for always telling me that I could do it. For watching me get on a plane, and for welcoming me back. Thanks for always being there with a cup of tea at the end of the day. I may always suffer from small existential crises and want to run away to far-flung places in search of adventure and a bigger life. But every ship needs a harbour, and every harbour needs a lighthouse in a storm. Thanks for guiding me safely in.

Introduction

I start the slow and methodical process of wiping myself down. First the face, taking very little care to dry behind my ears as usual. Next, the shoulders and the arms. I drag the threadbare towel with the assured purpose that comes with years of practice and routine. Chest and tummy, before gripping an end in each hand and shimmying it across my back. Flicking it to the front again, I wipe down each leg with careful consideration so as not to graze the floor, and yet banish away every last cold drop still clinging to my prickly skin. The mirror is still foggy with steam from my lavish and long shower. I marvel at the genuine luxury of hot water, albeit from an electronic showerhead with wires visibly exposed. It's been a long week of too many cold showers; I don't even mind the barely-trickling water pressure.

As I pull on my baggy, soft cotton pants and t-shirt (my backpacker's substitute for flannel pajamas) and sneak back across the hallway, I regard the wooden stairwell and lime-coloured walls with a new curiosity. I walk slowly, to take it all in. Here I am on the other side of the world; showered, dried, warm and about to snuggle into a fluffy, queen-sized bed.

Clean. Safe. Tired. In Paraguay!

Utterly alone.

The benign and comfortable existence I'd been living at home was both a privilege and a prison, of sorts. Not for the first time on this trip, I longed for the routine of work and weekends (ok, maybe not work), of brunch with my husband, of nights curled on the couch and lazily staring at the television. I missed the picture-postcard views from our bedroom window and the creature comforts such as my little four-door hatchback and its ability to zip me to the beach or the shops (or the other end of the country, should it take my fancy!) I missed the ease of it all. The effortlessness of suburban life. And yet, in my cozy existence, I felt suffocated. A growing darkness pressed ever more heavily on my shoulders, surrounding me from all sides, creeping into the most comfortable of places. Sucking away my happiness.

Call it your typical 'Gen Y' sense of entitlement and itchy feet, but the more I buried my head in books about daring adventures in treacherous places, the more I longed to leave my life of moderate ease; fancying myself some sort of modern day Indiana Jones (albeit with a can of hairspray and a jar of bronzer in tow). Every 'problem' that snuck its way into my whirring mind from absolute obscurity seemed to have but one answer: travel. But not just any kind of travel. No air-conditioned tour bus, no guided city walks and down-to-the-hour schedules. I didn't want to plod along in single-file, tripping over the heels of the obnoxious red-faced tourist in front of me, to witness a well-rehearsed spiel from a 'local expert' about the historical significance of (*insert historically significant attraction here*). No. The more I puttered away at daily life, getting more and more comfortable, creeping ever so slowly towards middle age, the more I wanted to be somewhere *other than here*. The more I wanted to experience something *other than this*. The more I wanted simply, *otherness*.

1

The Black Cat

The door stuck as I pushed against it. I tried again (*once more with feeling*) and it burst open with a judder. Inside I found a dimly lit room sparsely furnished with a waiting chair, a refrigerator (well stocked with beer, I dutifully noted) and a reception desk littered with papers. Casting a glimpse into the room beyond, I caught shades of green and a smattering of sunlight which suggested the leafy courtyard I'd read about in the online reviews. All at once I was scared, curious and excited. I approached the desk.

Only a few months ago I'd plotted, planned and dreamed with three friends; or more accurately, one friend and two acquaintances, about our upcoming adventure to the other side of the world. Only a few days ago however, earlier plans having fallen apart, I'd boarded the plane full of all the giddiness and naivety of the younger person I'd once been, and hoped to be again; if only for a few short weeks. Trying desperately to find adventure and meaning in an increasingly mundane existence, I'd foregone several of my less practical outfits and much bathroom paraphernalia. I had managed to squeeze, cull and force all of my *essential* belongings down to a tidy, 12 kg package which would represent my worldly possessions for the next four weeks. Leaving a worrying (albeit begrudgingly supportive) husband behind, I'd given a teary goodbye and practically raced to the departure lounge bar to enjoy a first holiday champagne with my now sole travelling companion, Karen. The world, or at least, the vast expanse of South America, was to be our proverbial oyster.

Somewhere in the days that followed, it had all gone to pieces. Three friends down to one, and now, none. I found myself alone in a foreign country, with no more than a scrap of badly pronounced words in the local language and only a vague idea of what I would do next. About to embark on an unplanned solo backpacking trek throughout this strange and (possibly) dangerous place, I had never felt more vulnerable. The world around me had never felt so … *other*.

The Black Cat Hostel was Trip Adviser's best-rated accommodation in the colonial town of Asunción, Paraguay. It was also one of the few which, according to the booking website, had an available private room for the next three nights. The approximate amount of time, I figured, that I needed in order to relax, regroup, figure out what the HELL I was going to do for the next three and a half weeks and how the HECK I was going to do it alone.

Of all my (limited) travelling adventures, this was sure to be the most noteworthy. For all of the right reasons, I hoped.

"Hi!" I chirped nervously, English-to-Spanish dictionary in hand. "Aaahhh ... *Hay habitaciones libres?*"

"Yes, we have rooms available. Would you like private or dorm?" the receptionist replied, in English. (Thank GOODNESS!)

My understanding of Spanish, I had recently learned, was not only terribly lacking in depth but was an almost unrecognisable slaughtering of pronunciation. When I'd tried to order a packet of cheese and onion flavoured chips at the bus depot in Buenos Aires (*"cebolla and aaaah queso?"*), the pre-pubescent stall attendant had been so kind to point out to me,

"Your Spanish ... very bad."

Rather than retort, I simply grinned sheepishly, paid for my chips and left. Defeated. My grasp of foreign languages may have been abysmal, but at least I always gave it my best shot.

My ex-travelling companion, Karen, had a thick New Zealand accent which the Argentinians we'd encountered found extremely difficult to decipher (as did I, at times). Not only this, but she absolutely refused to learn or utter a single word of Spanish, not so much as a *"por favour"* or *"gracias"*. Not a word. Zilch. Nothing. I'd found this particularly irritating and frankly, one of the typical displays of behaviour which makes tourists thoroughly unlikeable just about anywhere in the world. I should have known, from the moment I introduced the idea of learning a little bit of Spanish via an app I'd downloaded on my phone. I was visiting Karen for dinner, to hash out some more of our 'wish list' for the trip. The wish list was in lieu of actual plans, as we'd decided that

7

we needed the freedom of being able to take our time, enjoy ourselves and experience each place for as long as we deemed necessary. When I showed the new app to Karen, she shooed me away with a laugh and passed me another glass of wine. *Ce la vie!* You only live once, right?

That afternoon at the Black Cat, having paid for my (enormous) private room (shared bathroom, but hey, you have to slum it sometimes!) and unpacked a few things, I'd taken my book and gone to sit down by the tiny plunge pool in the aforementioned leafy courtyard. It's true what they say about hostels, that you cannot find a better way to meet people. Staying in a hotel, I've found, you will rarely encounter any meaningful conversation beyond obligatory niceties and greetings. I had barely opened to my book-marked page and glanced down to start reading when I heard the ubiquitous hostel greeting, *"Hey, where are you from?"* in some nondescript European accent. Oh good, I thought, I'm clearly giving off the *don't-try-speaking-Spanish-to-me-as-you-will-be-sorely-disappointed* look. I can't say I was surprised, or upset about this. Looking up, I was presented with a large, slightly-sunburnt man sporting a shock of blond hair and an altogether too-large silver chain around his neck. I had to quickly stifle a groan when I recognised the international symbol he was wearing for 'I'm a loud beer-swilling tourist'; a Bintang singlet. I would have been wary, frightened even, if he hadn't had the round, pink face of an overgrown toddler and an ever-so-slightly dopey grin.

"I'm from Australia!" I offered, grinning back despite myself, and squinting a little in the sunshine.

"AH! AUSTRALIA! KYLIE MINOGUE, eh?" he bellowed. *(This may not be a completely accurate recollection on my part. However, every time that I mentioned I was Australian it would rouse a response of this kind or similar.)*

"We are going down to the beach in a few minutes," he continued. "You want to come with us? Me and my buddies?"

A lone female tourist should perhaps be wary of these kinds of invitations, or at least have an idea who these 'mates' are before she agrees to it. But I was a bold, audacious, intrepid backpacker now! Up for some adventure, some new experiences, some sunbaking with strangers and frankly, some companionship; now that I was alone and indeed a little bit lonely in my new surroundings.

"Sure!" I chimed, wariness be damned! "Let me go and get my swimmers!"

Never mind that Paraguay is a land-locked country, and is as likely to have a 'beach' as Rwanda or Slovakia. Tiny details, I thought! *Tiny details!* And so, I was off to the *beach*. In my swimmers. With a group of five lads whom I'd never met, and a sense of adventure that I'd rarely felt before now. *Emocionante!*

2

An Exercise in Planned Insanity – The Great Ocean Road

I'd read about 'Great Walks' around the world for years, and I'd always been fascinated by the idea of moving at a snail's pace (approximately the speed at which I walk) through beautiful scenery, which is so easy to miss by car, train or coach. Paula Constant's *Sahara* had piqued my interest initially, followed by *Tracks* by Robyn Davidson. It was perhaps Dervla Murphy though, who really cemented in my mind the idea of treading the footpaths of the world with meagre possessions on your back (although, in her case, in her panniers; you see, she cycled around the world in *Full Tilt: Ireland to India with a Bicycle*).

For some reason, I had believed Dervla had died in Syria on her last round-the-world cycling adventure. However, upon closer inspection it appears she is still alive and (presumably) well, living in Ireland at the age of 83. I don't know what lead me to believe she had died; I do have a terrible memory and tend to jumble my facts. Nonetheless, this mistaken understanding of a tragic end to her adventures only spurred me on and lifted my interest. What better way to leave the world after decades of adventures than to kick the proverbial bucket in some far-flung land, doing what you love and chasing the next escapade into madness!

As a bit of an armchair explorer myself, I'd always dreamed of travelling in a more basic, unsophisticated and rudimentary way. Without all of the bells and whistles of hotels and air-conditioned coaches, I figured there would be more opportunity to really see, smell, touch and taste the places I was exploring. Since my South American trip, I was now firmly a converted hotel-dweller; preferring to stay in cheap hostels without so much as reliable hot water let alone miniature shampoo, conditioner and body wash in the bathrooms. I'd learned in my limited experience that the best part of any holiday is always the people I meet along the way (dodgy Bolivian travel agents notwithstanding – but more about that later). As I knew now, there is no better way to meet people properly than to be sharing space in a dingy establishment on the other side of the world and striking up a conversation over a dodgy local beer and an empanada.

Finally, through with couch-sitting and daydreaming, I came up with the harebrained idea of hiking the Great Ocean Walk in the south of Victoria. This 104-km trek would take me past some of the most beautiful stretches of the Australian coastline; much of it inaccessible by car. I contacted my Melbournian friend, Bec (who, incidentally is always up for just about anything and is generally unflappable) and without so much as a 'hmmmm let me think about it' she was on board. Flights booked; gear researched, scrutinised for weight, bought, and packed; and trail food discussed and decided upon – we were off!

Perhaps the next best part of any holiday is the planning. Researching ultralight gear and reading forum after forum of intrepid long-hikers was exhilarating in itself. Getting to learn and then use the lingo (ultra-lite hexamine portable stove, 'vitamin I', framed versus unframed packs, top loading versus side, dehydrated chicken curry, water purification tablets versus portable filtration system) made me feel like a pro. Before we knew it, we had our topographical map, were analysing inclines and altitudes, and pulling on our packs for the first steps of the trip.

Worryingly, within moments of donning my 20-kg pack, my feet started to go numb. I'd hiked many times before, but never overnight (let alone for a week straight!), and carrying all of the gear was really sending my feet into conniptions. Despite all of my research, it seems I was unprepared physically for the demands of the walk; and we'd barely begun! Bec was a novice, having never hiked before, and I didn't want to make her panic before we'd even really begun, so I downplayed my discomfort. Better numb than bleeding, right?

Much to our displeasure, the sleepy seaside village of Apollo Bay had only one taxi driver, and he was currently out of town on a fare. This meant that before we'd even reached the starting point of the hike at the Apollo Bay Information Centre, we had to hike 12 to 13 ks to town from our car park. Our moderate 10 km first day turned into closer to 23 ks and it only got worse as the day wore on. My feet were extremely unhappy, but they were soon joined in their protestations by my legs. Steep ascents and descents meant that my poor, chubby little pegs were working overtime to haul my already overweight ass plus 20 kg of pack up and down hills and ravines. Within three hours I'd pulled a groin muscle on my right side and my leg damn near refused to move. We'd passed by amazing beach crossings and crystalline inlets of the freshest and most intoxicatingly beautiful water; and I'd half ignored them all as I struggled simply to put one aching foot in front of the other. Climbing from a final beach crossing (fuck you, soft, golden sand!) and starting one last seemingly never-ending ascent into the bush, I just about lied down and died right there. The only thing that prevented me from crumbling into a sweaty ball of pain and fury and tears was the simple fact that this would suck yet more energy out of me. I was reduced to crab-style sideways walking up each hill at literally crawling pace, due to my right leg steadfastly refusing to cooperate. Finally, I crossed some other walkers heading downhill who'd come through for a day-hike (lucky fuckers), who told me that Bec wasn't too far up ahead, enquired about my welfare and wished to inform me that the campsite was not 'too far' away.

Bec had been killing it all day. Having never so much as strapped on a pair of hiking shoes before, she was putting me to shame and practically skipping along the track. I wanted to murder her and then eat her remains. Extreme! This was the nature of my mental state. Soon enough (though it felt like hours to me) her beaming face came bounding down the hill, carrying the rest of her still-perky body with her. I gave her a look that all at once said,

'I'm glad you're still feeling chipper; I want to kill you; I'm about three minutes away from slitting my own throat with my multi-tool knife; please fucking tell me that the goddam campsite is just around this fucking corner.'

Interpreting my expression accurately, she cheerfully took my pack from me and bounded back up the hill, telling me I was 'nearly there'. Now, if I ever hear those goddam words come from someone's mouth again, I'm likely to involuntarily slap them in some PTSD-induced red mist of rage. I dragged my sorry ass and mangled right leg up that hill for minute after excruciating minute, for what felt like an age. 'Nearly there' my ass! Every time we came to another bend in the track, I thought, surely, SURELY this is it, only to be sorely disappointed with yet more featureless bush land and scrub. Plodding along, putting one battered foot in front of the other, I thought, if I never see another eucalypt again …

Finally, and despite every cell in my body telling me that this was some cruel, intergalactic joke by a bunch of bored alien overlords to torture me into madness, the sign came into view.

Camping by permit only. Hike-in Campsites ➜

Oh Holy Spaghetti Monster and all that is good in this world: THANK YOU! With a few dozen more painful steps (just for shits and giggles, on behalf of Parks Victoria, I'm sure) the first shelter came slowly into view. Bec had, of course, already checked out each of the eight individual campsites in her ample time skipping around and had sussed out the best pick of the bunch.

Setting up camp was decidedly more pleasant than the last few hours of turmoil, and brought back memories of childhood camping expeditions with Dad. There's something innately satisfying about setting up a shelter (in my case, ultralight one-man tent), unpacking gear and boiling a billy of water for the day's first cup of tea. It gives me a serene sense of being capable, fearless and self-sufficient. Despite all of my moaning and grumbling throughout that awful, torturous day, I felt accomplished and fulfilled as I sat down with my collapsible rubber cup in hand, tea bag dangling in the breeze. How fickle my temper can be, I thought to myself.

We had not long been set up when we heard other hikers approach the communal shelter, and as Bec went to refill her camelback pouch, she investigated. They were an older couple, perhaps in their 50s. Having rested, my muscles began to seize in that *'now that you're good and relaxed, I'm just going to start to bother you some more'* way, and I hobbled over to fill my own pouch and meet the 'newcomers'. I have to admit to feeling quite proud of the fact that we'd been the first to arrive, despite our mammoth day and extra unexpected kilometres. I must have looked like some kind of mad-woman or gargoyle as I stumbled and groaned towards the water tank and shelter. Despite my zombie-like appearance, I was met with a beaming smile by a bloke who introduced himself as Graham, as he studiously unpacked gear from a large pack. Suzanne, his partner, was sitting in the shelter in a somewhat compromised position; removing her hiking pants. I grinned at her and shrugged as if to say 'you gotta do what you gotta do!' and she grinned back, a little embarrassed perhaps, but continued with the job.

We chatted briefly as I filled up from the water tank and popped a couple of purification tablets into the pouch. Turns out they'd seen us on our walk towards the information centre earlier that day; they'd started later as the day was only a 'short one'. They'd commenced their trek from the *proper* starting place, and both appeared to be experienced hikers. We swapped war stories about the steep inclines that day, and I was glad to hear that they'd found it really challenging as well. We then wished each other a peaceful night's sleep, and retired to our tents.

A good night's sleep it was not – for me at least. My aching muscles played havoc all night, and I tossed and turned like a feverish baby. I woke early the next morning feeling both unrested and yet eager to get up and off the hard ground. It had been a cold and breezy night, despite being camped well into the bush and away from the coast. After breakfast (porridge with dehydrated milk for me; *Oats To Go* popper for Bec), we lazily repacked gear and generally stuffed around. Suzanne and Graham had already hit the frog and toad ('the road' for you non-Aussies) to get an early start.

My pulled groin muscle was already giving me grief and I knew that any uphill climbs that day would prove to be near impossible. Something had to be done. As I packed my gear I considered my options and eventually came up with a MacGyver-esque solution. I pulled a spare Occy strap around the back of the leg in question and strapped it to the front of my bum-bag (once again, for the non-Australians, that's an Octopus strap – stretchy band of rope not dissimilar to a bungee cord). It sat tight and comfortably, and meant that every time I lifted my foot from the ground my leg would spring forward with very little effort from the muscles affected. Brilliant! I trudged along that day (which thankfully was much more mild than the first) and my leg gave me very little grief. Huzzah!

As we stopped about half way for a snack and a bush-toilet break for Bec, we were approached by a group of four men. They were a little older than us, perhaps late 30s. As we made space for them on the bench, we started the usual round of conversations between hikers: Where have you come from? Where are you going? How long are you hiking for? How shit was today?

One of them spotted the Occy strap around my leg; on which I'd unwittingly left the bright yellow tag (and which embarrassingly sat right at crotch-level; good one, idiot), and asked me what that was about. I explained my predicament of my pulled muscle and how the strap worked to counter it. To my surprise, they all seemed quite impressed at my ingenuity. Even more impressed, when they learned that we were doing the full hike from start to finish over a week. We'd certainly gained some trail-cred. I was chuffed and buoyed by their awe, and left shortly after with a slight spring in my (still awkward) step.

The track ran roughly uphill for the first half and downhill for the second. We learned that day how deceptive the distances can be when you don't have regular signposts to indicate how far you've come. Or more importantly, how far you've got to go. When we started to head downhill finally, I was very relieved, so too was my leg. We hiked for what felt like miles and miles and yet, around every bend where we expected to see a sign for the campsite, we were left disappointed, and greeted with yet more bush. Finally, we reached a beach crossing and confirmed with the map that indeed, this would be the last leg of the day before we made it to camp. It really didn't look far on the map, and yet we should have known better. Even though we were novice map-readers, we still had an idea of the scale and the time it had taken to make it that far. Walking on sand is no picnic at the best of times, let alone when carrying what is effectively a small person on your back. My leg had, as yet, coped well that day with my ad hoc solution; however, the sand was not so easily thwarted. Piercing blows of pain shot through the muscle with each step, and as we rounded bend after bend of beachfront, I once again considered sitting down and letting the wildlife lay waste to my broken body.

Bec negotiated each corner well ahead of me with ease and I caught occasional glimpses of a boot or a backpack as she flitted along over sand and rock and pool. The terrain became alien and strange. Sand turned to large, sharp, bizarre rock slices. Pools of water and dark, sinister looking seaweed clotted between the coils of this peculiar stone. Carefully and slowly I picked my way over each mound, mindful of the sharp edges and unpleasant injuries that lay in wait, should I slip. At last, I rounded the final corner of the Martian landscape of this beach and could see the familiar yellow blaze of a trail sign. There were two of them. One, a few hundred yards beyond the other. I caught up to Bec and asked her which blaze we should follow. The second one, she assured me, was our campsite and saviour. We trudged through the last few hundred metres and up yet another steep set of stairs back into the bush. Eventually we came across a sign 'Camping by permit only' and a boot-washing station. We must be close. Hurray!

We weren't. Damn it. Following little more than a goat-track, we walked on and on and on. There were no more signs. No campsite. I was beginning, again, to lose hope. I was beginning, again, to get a little melodramatic in my inner monologue. I rounded the bend and found Bec sitting atop a rock, map in hand.

"You're not going to like this…"

There was a long pause while I said nothing.

"We have to go back to that first sign. We've missed the campsite."

Fuckinghellareyoufuckingkiddingme?Imgoingtofuckin gkillsomebody!
Probablyyoujustbecauseyouretheonlypersonclosee-noughtokill!

I didn't utter a word. At least not audibly. I simply sighed, turned around and began to head back down the maddening little goat-track I'd just followed for God knows how long. Bec shot ahead, as usual, no doubt hoping to get back to the actual campsite and then come back bearing news of my imminent arrival, lest I lose my mind out there at any moment.

For the first time on that trip, I began to cry. Not consciously or with intent, tears began to stream down my dirt-crusted cheeks uncontrollably. I silently sobbed the pathetic sob of someone who, with their whole heart, wants to lie down and die. If it weren't for the giant ants exploring the path, I may have done just that. My tears defied me and continued to fall as I resigned myself to my fate and tried to simply leave my body and watch it from above in existential despair. Putting one foot agonisingly in front of the other, I continued. Back down the little track. Back down onto the beach. Back across the seaweed and sand. Back to that first signpost that we'd foolishly ignored and walked straight past.

As I approached the top of yet another set of stairs from the beach, I could make out a clearing and the unmistakable outline of a camp shelter. There were a number of people gathered under the roof in the late afternoon warmth, enjoying a cup of tea or a snack. As I approached, looking for Bec, I felt their eyes upon me. I felt broken and ashamed and utterly exhausted. It felt as though each of them had been briefed on our near-miss of the campsite, on my overwhelming lack of fitness and preparedness for this hike, on my absolute and total weakness of character. I barely made eye contact with any of them as I passed, although I registered that Suzanne and Graham, as well as the four men we'd met earlier that day were among them. How completely embarrassed and unworthy I felt among this group of accomplished and capable hikers.

I found Bec setting up in one of the sites. She knew better than to approach me with cheery chit-chat, or to ask me how I was feeling. She simply let me lay down my pack and, in silence, begin to set up my tent. Once I was done, I finally sat down to remove my shoes. This was left until last on purpose, as once those shoes came off, they were not going back on again. My feet immediately swelled and began to throb. I could see that they were swollen to well beyond their normal size. I was not surprised. I barely registered the aching. Looking over to Bec, I felt as though each of us had been having a silent argument with the other for the last couple of hours. Me with her, for having assured me we take the second blaze, and for being wrong and causing me further despair. Her with me, for being so useless and helpless and bereft of enjoyment for this trip. I offered a white flag of peace and surrender with a shrug and a sideways grin, so as to suggest that I knew how useless and hopeless I was. It said 'Hey! What a fucker of a day. Thank fuck we are both here. Let us never speak about today's events again.'

"Cup of tea?" I said, aloud this time.

She smiled. "Yes please!"

3

Death By Blisters –
The Great Ocean Walk continued

That night I stayed up late, chatting with the other hikers in camp. It was a much larger group that night and as well as Suzanne, Graham and 'The Four Blokes', we had a father-daughter couple and another gentleman; whose names I have since forgotten. This is not a reflection of their less-than-memorable characters, simply of my foggy brain and poor head for names.

That night was perhaps the most memorable and influential of the week, for me at least. Bec had shot off to bed early, as is often the way with a hiker, when you're out under the stars and the sun has disappeared. As I hadn't slept well the night before, I thought that perhaps staying up later might help to make me good and tired before bed.

Suzanne regaled us with stories of her Camino – a hike I'd long dreamed of taking. 800 ks through the South of France and across Spain. Camino de Santiago de Compostella. She and Graham had met on the French Camino and Graham was heading off in less than a month to complete the Spanish one himself. Hearing stories of other hikes comes with the territory when you're on a Great Walk, and it's without a doubt my favourite part. Methodically setting up camp each night, eating an early dinner and then sitting back with a cup of tea and a group of fellow walkers is one of the most satisfying and heart-warming of evenings one can have. Suzanne was clearly an accomplished, no-nonsense kind of woman. Initially I had worried that she might find my struggles trivial and weak. Hopeless even. The night we'd met at the first campsite she'd been quiet and almost cool, while Graham had done most of the talking. But tonight, over war stories of blisters and strained muscles, she warmed to me and opened up. I felt a real camaraderie between us, and rather than shake her head and dismiss my struggles she sympathised, advised and encouraged me. 'It happens to us all,' she said. And I knew that she meant it. I didn't need to be an expert. This was my first big hike, and a tough one to cut my teeth on. At least I was out here chasing an adventure (when I could be on a beach, sipping a daiquiri. Heaven forbid!)

When I'd mentioned to Suzanne that I enjoyed meeting people on my holidays almost more than I enjoyed the sights and tastes and sounds of a new place, she'd immediately removed a layer of outward coolness. Her eyes lit up in the waning light and I knew I'd found a kindred spirit. After all, she had met Graham on a Great Walk. Clearly she shared my opinion on this matter. We talked until well into the night, after the sun had long set and we were the last to head to our tents to curl up.

After a sheet or so of ibuprofen and codeine that night, I slept much better. I like to think it was the good

conversation and later bed time that did it, but the damp-
ened aching of muscles and joints probably had more to
do with it. I rose early the next morning with a view to
watching the sun come up, however I wasn't quite early
enough for that. Bec had been down to check out the beach
already, and I busied myself cleaning my teeth and prepar-
ing my morning staple of porridge and dehydrated milk.
I was feeling sore and battered but well slept, at least, and
I hoped that today my muscles and poor feet might start
to have built up a resistance to the strain they were under.

By some temporary madness, we'd decided to make
this third day a long one by skipping Cape Otway campsite and heading on to Aire River. Now that we had map
in hand which outlined the steep climb and descents we
could expect, as well as beach crossings and a myriad of
other tiny trials designed to drive me insane, I was more
than a little worried about whether I'd make it there. I
figured that if I could at least make it to the lighthouse
at Cape Otway, I'd be close enough to civilisation to seek
help and/or rescue if necessary.

The day started out easily enough, traipsing
through the bush and keeping an eye out for koalas in the
trees. We'd seen a couple here and there. To be honest,
it was Bec who was looking out for wildlife, whereas I
was merely registering a polite interested glance when she
pointed them out to me while trying to concentrate on not
thinking about how much my feet hurt. Every time I saw
a climb or rise coming into view I'd try to kid myself that
it wouldn't be too difficult and couldn't possibly last long.
There really wasn't any other viable option (I didn't count
'lie down and cry' as an option by this stage, although it

did sit there in the back of my mind as a last, last, very last resort.)

We'd left well before The Four Blokes that morning, although it didn't take them long to catch up to us once they set off. They went at a cracking pace and put me to shame. I could sense that Bec wished she could pick up the back of their procession and follow along at a pace more suited to her abilities. I was holding her back, and while she was ever patient and accommodating, I felt as though she needed a chance to crack on and really test herself out. She was really excelling at this hiking malarkey that she'd 'never tried before' and she loved to challenge herself. She was too polite to mention it to me, but through my guilt and helplessness I was all too aware of my shortcomings and hyper aware of the vibe she was giving off.

We came to a steep descent which eventually led – painfully – to a beach crossing. The secluded inlet we found ourselves stepping out from was possibly one of the most magnificent spots I'd ever encountered. Clear, aquamarine waters lapped lazily against the sand and trickled into rock pools around the edges where the beachfront met with the bush. It was a gorgeous blue-sky day and a cool 12 or 15 degrees celsius under the glorious sun. The guys were spread out for an early lunch in a shady spot, a couple of them taking a dip in the waters. It looked amazing and I envied them so. I really wanted to rush over to them (or hobble, as it were) and sit down for a snack, a swim and a lazy nap in the sun. Alas, I knew that we were already struggling for time on this huge day, and at my pace we'd be lucky to make it by sunset. I was moving so slowly, and we had so far to go, that I was missing out on the sights and experiences that had been my reasons for wanting to come. I was too exhausted to even stop, take out my camera and snap a few shots to reflect upon in hindsight. I was struggling so much that I truly was missing the beauty of the trip.

I gave a dejected wave to the boys and persisted along the beach towards the next blaze. I followed the trail that led back into the trees and let out an audible gasp – but only briefly. I could see the huge, steep, winding trail of stone steps following the coastline up a vast, almost vertical cliff. My gasp was brief because I knew instantly, almost before the sound had left my mouth that this was a point at which I really, truly might actually give up. That hill was almost inconceivably high. The left side of my brain gave me a bollocking and demanded that I steel myself and simply move up there, one Goddamn step at a time. The right side however, was secretly and quietly cursing the day I'd ever heard the words, 'Great. Ocean. Walk'. While it was at it, it was running an inner slide-reel of happy snaps outlining what I *could* be doing right now instead of the motherfucking hike. At home napping. Watching a movie. Out for lunch. God, even working would be better than this current situation. Nothing for it, the left-side brain won out and I made a bee line for the stairs.

Bec turned briefly around to check on my progress and once I'd waved her off with an, 'I know. It's going to be fucked. You just go ahead and I'll see you in a few hours' look, she disappeared around the first bend. There was naught left to do but start, and so I lifted my left foot and made contact with the very first limestone step. There, that wasn't so bad. Another step. And another. Never mind that I had to steady myself, adjust my pack and move all of my weight to the other leg before I could take each stride. At this rate, it really would take me hours to make it up there. Perhaps mercifully, I couldn't see more than 20 or 30 steps at a time, as the trail curved and the rest of the path was obscured. If I can just make it to the top of the next bend, I'm sure I'll be almost there, I thought. I can't tell you how many times I had to say that to myself, as though spurring on a small child with unconvincing lies and propaganda. Each time I made another rise, I'd turn a corner and see yet more stairs. Never-ending stairs. I could occasionally get a peek through the trees and back down to the beach where the boys were still relaxing. If they'd just stay there for another hour or two, and then climb the stairs more slowly than they'd done any other stretch of this hike, then I might, *might* just make it to the top before they came across me.

The only thing less bearable than the stairs at that stage, was the thought that I might be passed by those damned capable, intrepid walkers, who would look on me with pity and disgust as they saw my face, mangled into a grimace of pain and exhaustion. It would literally be adding insult to injury and I realised that it was a cliché for a reason.

On one or two occasions I passed yet another bend and saw Bec sitting peacefully against a rock or atop a stair, just waiting long enough to see that I was still alive before heading further up. I couldn't manage a smile, but I gave her a shrug and a half-hearted wave each time. I wanted her to know that I was just getting on with the job. That I wasn't giving up. That I wasn't lying down and crying. That I wasn't an awful, pitiful, useless lump of sweat and fat and oily hair.

Against all odds, I finally saw that miraculous rise. There didn't appear to be another bend, there was clear air and nothing else beyond those stairs. Not more trees. Not more track. Not more agonising climbing. Was it a mirage? A trick of the light? A result of delirium? Bec was standing there taking photos, pack on the ground beside her. She didn't move along again once she saw me. This must be it.

It was.

I very nearly sat down and bawled like the big baby I was. Instead, I contented myself with sitting, gulping down some water and resting my feet. As was to be expected, they began to throb immediately. My toes pushed against the insides of my shoes. My arches ached and strained against the laces and tongue that held them in place. They were not a happy pair of feet, and we hadn't even made it to Cape Otway yet. According to the map, that was still another few kilometres away. We'd only made it 3 or 4 ks that day so far and it had taken *hours.* How on earth was I going to make it to Aire River, another 10 or 12 ks past Cape Otway? It may as well have been one hundred miles. Two hundred. There was no way my feet would make it.

I'd had barely five minutes to contemplate this when The Four Blokes arrived. Even they looked tired this time. A couple of them had even broken a visible sweat. Instead of disgust and pity, they greeted me with pats on the back and enquiries as to the welfare of my feet. 'They're stuffed,

I think,' I told them. 'I don't even know how they made it up that hill.'

What happened next changed the course of the hike for both Bec and I. 'We are going to Cape Otway where our car is parked, and then driving home,' one of them said. 'We can get the car, come back and get you, and take you on to Aire River?'

Oh Holy Christ! I could not believe my ears. I had not even realised it, but the top of the hill (and that term is used loosely; the thing we'd just climbed was damn near a mountain) was actually a car park and a small campsite. I tried to contain my excitement and not jump on their offer too greedily. They were keen to press on, I could see, and I didn't want to waste this opportunity. My pride went out the window.

"That … would be amazing. But I really don't want to put you out. Is it very far out of your way?"

"Don't be silly. It isn't far at all."

He was right. Any distance by car seemed like a breeze after you've had to struggle every inch for the last three days. They agreed to come back and get me; Bec would hike on with them to Cape Otway and then onto Aire River by herself. We had a mere few moments to organise this and to say our goodbyes. I didn't have time to contemplate whether this was a good idea for her or not. She was still in good shape and I knew she wouldn't have any trouble making it, but at what time? I hoped for her sake that it wasn't going to mean hiking in the dark. We each had head torches, but we didn't know what the terrain would be like, or how treacherous it might be in the dark. She seemed unfazed and happy to get going. In less than two minutes it was decided, and they were off, Bec among them, and me sitting alone atop a cliff, with nothing to do but wait. Wait and hope that I had understood correctly. Wait and hope that they wouldn't forget about me, get lost, or decide against taking the detour to come and pick me up. Wait and hope that I didn't encounter any serial killers in that secluded car park.

4

Bribing Border Guards (Paraguay)

Before arriving in Paraguay, I had dutifully consulted the Australian *Smart Traveller* website for tips on visas and entry requirements. The website had proven handy for researching the whole trip before leaving home, and I felt safe in the knowledge that most countries I planned on visiting didn't require an Aussie to organise anything in advance; just the kind of travel I liked! Unfortunately for me, within days of arriving in South America it had become obvious that travelling around by air to each destination would be well outside of my budget. There were only a few things on my 'must see' list, and the furthest of these was some 3000 ks away in Peru. A few late-night scribblings on the back of envelopes and I surmised that a lot of bus travel would be involved. No problem, I thought. I can rough in on a bus for a few hours. Huh! Famous last words, as this was well before I'd encountered the delights of Bolivian bus travel (more about that soon).

After a long and surprisingly comfortable bus ride (just another way to lure me into a false sense of security about my intrepidness and the reliability of South American travel) up to Iguazu Falls on the northern tip of Argentina, it was crunch time; I had to find a way to Bolivia and then onto Peru. Flying between major cities within each country was not bank-breakingly expensive; however, flying across borders was. It was going to cost upwards of AUD$800 to make it from Iguazu to Bolivia to Peru and I just didn't have that kind of cash to splash around. I made my way to the local travel agent in town, and in my best Spanish (which as you already know is mediocre; and that's putting it kindly) and his best English (which, albeit limited, was better than my Spanish) we muddled through until he understood what I was trying to achieve. He suggested a bus into Paraguay, and then later onto Santa Cruz, Bolivia. This wouldn't have been a problem – albeit a lot of hours spent in transit – except for the fact that I hadn't planned on visiting Paraguay and therefore wasn't sure about the entry requirements for Australians. The *Smart Traveller* website was spectacularly unhelpful on this particular issue and simply suggested that travellers 'consult with Paraguayan officials'. Bit late for that. I expressed my concern via a multitude of sign language attempts and several scribbled notes, while pointing at my passport. The travel agent seemed to understand, once again (bless him!) what I was on about and decided to 'phone a friend' for some advice.

I have no idea who this friend was, or on what authority he seemed to be operating but I was assured that 'the friend' was most adamant that Australians did not need visas to enter Paraguay. Right, well, that settled it then; and I bought my bus ticket for later that very same day. Waiting at the bus depot, I was nervous about not seeing my bus or somehow being trapped in the bathroom when it arrived and therefore missing it. All of those crazy thoughts that go through your mind when you're travelling to unknown places, with very little in the way of plans and even less in the way of the local language. I bought a cold drink from a nearby convenience store and planted my butt firmly at the platform where I'd been told the bus would arrive. There would be no ill-timed bathroom breaks for this lady! No, I wasn't moving until that thing arrived – bladder bursting or not.

I really needn't have worried, because when the bus finally arrived, the driver took his sweet time allowing all of the passengers to board, and puttered around in and out of the terminal (presumably to relieve and perhaps feed himself). All in all it took about an hour before we finally set off. Clearly marked on the front of the bus was the destination: Asunción, Paraguay. There didn't seem to be any other foreigners on board, and as people jumped on and off at seemingly random stops, I moved closer to the front so as to be able to consult with the bus driver, should I panic about where I needed to get off. Once again, I needn't have worried about the destination as we soon came upon what was very obviously a border crossing. I had heard a lot about Argentinians making trips to Paraguay to purchase electronic goods and the like, as the taxes there were much lower. I saw bus after bus zoom past the border in each direction, and as our bus passed the checkpoint I thought Huzzah! No visa required! On to Asunción!

So, it was to my dismay that several hundred metres past the checkpoint, the bus ground to a halt and the bus driver pointed first to me and then to the door. I stared back blankly. He pointed again, smiled, and pointed to my bag. Then he pointed back down the road to the border office. Oh fuck! Now what? He spoke exactly zero English and although I tried my darndest, I simply possessed neither the Spanish nor the sign language skills to ask him whether he was going to wait for me, how far it was to the town centre and whether I would need to somehow find another ride. There was really nothing for it but for me to hoist my backpack (not an easy task – and a lesson which I clearly had forgotten before attempting the Great Ocean Walk) and stumble on down the road, back to the checkpoint. Don't panic. Don't panic. For goodness sake, don't panic.

I made it to the office and through the automatic doors and was met with a welcome, cool room, large and bare, with but a few desks at the far end and a row of empty chairs against the wall. Officious-looking men sat behind a handful of officious-looking desks and I approached cautiously, with my best 'please let me into your country' wary smile on my face. In what I hoped was a *not-too-confident-yet-not-too-scared* kind of air, I produced my passport and uttered a friendly 'hola'. He flicked through the pages and stamps in my passport apparently in search of something that was not there, for he got to the end and proceeded to flick through it again, more slowly. Fuck, fuck, fu¿Visa?" he asked. Fuckity fuck! Calm. Be Calm.

"Australian,' I said. 'Don't need visa!" I flashed him a big smile. Confidence will out, yeah?

"Australian. Visa. Where visa?"

Oh for Pete's sake! Really? I launched into a part-Spanish-part-English-part-sign-language explanation of how the guy at the travel agent's had called a friend, and that friend had assured me that I didn't need a visa, and that now I was here and without a visa, and I needed to get through and PLEASE DON'T MAKE ME GO ALL THE WAY BACK TO BUENOS AIRES BECAUSE THAT WOULD TAKE TWO DAYS EACH WAY!

Nonplussed, he simply stared back at me, stony-faced. I'm not sure whether he couldn't understand me. Or worse, understood me perfectly and quite simply couldn't care less.

"You go back to Buenos Aires and get visa. Come back then."

I considered lying down on the floor and letting the wave of panic rush over me until I was a bawling, heaving mass of crying, dust-encrusted mush. But that wouldn't have got me anywhere. Except maybe locked up. Rather than melt into the tiles beneath me in a puddle of tears and hopelessness, I rallied my strength and put on my old favourite, *don't-fuck-with-me face's* close cousin, *I-can-do-this* face.

"Yes. Visa. You give me visa. How much?" I stared straight at him, with a falsely confident smile and a steely glare. For good measure, I threw in the money-fingers gesture and ever so slightly raised my left eyebrow, conspiratorially. Now I had his attention. He called over his mate from the neighbouring desk, who instantly grinned and, I imagine, pictured himself counting out his crisp new USD$ notes. Whatever the fee he had in mind, I didn't care, so long as it didn't include a stint in prison. I was verging on blind panic but had no choice but to act calm, like I did this kind of thing all the time. We can do business, gents. There's a price for everything. I kept it together long enough for Goon #1 and Goon #2 to have a quick chat, before Goon #2 looked up and fulfilled his part of the bargain …

"Yes, visa. Fifty US dollarsssss." He grinned, greedily. I'm sure he almost rubbed his pudgy little fingers together, but thought better of it. Clearly, Goon #2 was called in for situations that required a marginally better grasp of English, for sucker gringos like me. I was on to a winner though, and was more than happy to part with $50 to overcome this hurdle. As I handed over the cash, Goon #1 asked me, 'How long you want?'

I thought for a moment, before asking for three days. Cheerily, he took back my passport, stamped it and then hand wrote – HAND WROTE – '5 *dias tourista visa*' around the edge of the stamp. I couldn't make this shit up. I had a handwritten, dodgy tourist visa. Not only that, but the generous chap had given me an extra two whole fake days on my fake visa, so thrilled was he with my ample bribing prowess.

5

Sex Pests in Paraguay

The gang at The Black Cat Hostel grew over several days and soon we looked like a bar joke; an Aussie girl, a gay Bolivian, a pasty Brit, a young, handsome Dutchman, a suave Brazilian and a few other rag tag crew. We hung out on the makeshift rooftop terrace drinking beers from the hostel's fridge and talking travel, visas and the red tape involved with purchasing and riding motorcycles between South American nations.

The beach I'd been invited to within minutes of arriving at the hostel turned out to be a pebbly, dirty muck lining the banks of the Paraguay River which runs along the edge of the city. The group of guys and I had laid ourselves out on towels in the blistering heat and got to know each other. Rick, who'd been the one to invite me, clearly thought of himself as the leader of the bunch. He had a false bravado and from years in sales, I quickly picked out the bullshit gene in him; his inclination to tell tall tales and generally just talk absolute shit. I decided he was harmless, but that I wouldn't trust him with my grandmother. Harry, the shy Dutchman, was charming and softly spoken. He'd been in Paraguay for a few months already and had bought a motorcycle which he'd hoped to ride throughout South America. Turns out he couldn't even get it across the border due to some ridiculous bureaucratic nonsense and was stuck here until he could figure out what to do. He was handsome and young, with thick shoulder-length blond hair and typical Aryan blue eyes and tan. If it wasn't for his crippling shyness, he would have been an absolute lady killer. Mario was an effortlessly debonair Brazilian who was on a last-hurrah before heading to Argentina to open a juice bar with his beautiful wife. His easy manner, exquisite accent and clear yet subtle awareness of his own charisma reminded me of Rodrigo Santoro. In fact, they could have been brothers – the resemblance was uncanny.

We spent the afternoon lazing there on the 'beach' until somebody suggested beers and we all eagerly agreed to head back to the hostel for some rooftop lounging. Over the next few days we all spent time together intermittently. I was taught to cook a curry of some sort by an Indian guy who was also staying, and he showed me how to grocery shop here in Paraguay so that I didn't have to eat the only thing I could order in Spanish without being misunderstood; empanadas. For my final night in Paraguay it was decided that we should all go out to a local club down the street. It was also decided that we needed to go shopping for Harry, who had nothing to wear. Of course he had clothes to wear, but it was made apparent that this club was scheduled to be attended by a group of models that night, and as he hadn't so much as had a party-pash in his entire time in Paraguay, he wanted to look sharp. We all wanted to help the kid out.

Six of us braved the public transport system in order to make it to the local shopping centre. That was an adventure in itself, but by this stage I'd had my fair share of third-world-travel-nightmares. The shopping centre was much like any other in the world, with floors and floors of fashion, sporting and electronics stores. We wandered the menswear outlets for hours trying to find Harry something suitable. He was worse to shop with than any woman I'd ever met. He tried on pair after pair of jeans and shirt after shirt, and just could not make up his mind. In the end, after four hours of doubling back to revisit each store, he bought two overpriced shirts and a pair of designer jeans. Finally, we headed back to the hostel to get ready, and for Harry to have a shower.

I was hesitant to head out, as I hadn't been drinking or partying much since an epic red wine hangover in Buenos Aires. Not to mention, I had to fly out to Bolivia early the next morning and I really didn't need a groggy head for the trip. By this stage, another girl had checked in to our hostel and become a part of our little club. With her encouragement and wardrobe tips from Dimmi (the gay Bolivian who would have worn my heels if I'd let him), I was buoyed enough to venture out on the town. I had a beer downstairs in the common room with the others, while Paddy the Englishman played awful guitar in his underwear. In time, Harry made his grand entrance from the shower blocks and we all stopped, mouths open. It was like a scene from *Pretty Woman* as he sauntered down the stairs, all shiny and clean. He scrubbed up alright!

Understatement. He looked like a young Brad Pitt, blonde locks flowing and blow dried (where the heck did he get a blow dryer?) and new shirt and jeans on. He was ready to chat up some model folk and we all jumped in a cab.

Once inside the club, Rick handed me a cocktail. I wouldn't normally accept drinks that I hadn't ordered myself, however I was having a good time and was surrounded by friends. I took a few sips and handed the cocktail back to Rick. That is the last thing I remember for a while. My next clear memory is of falling out of a taxi in front of the Black Cat as the receptionist on nightshift hurried outside to help carry me in. He was a dead ringer for Billy Connolly, right down to the greying beard and Irish accent. Billy picked me up from the curb and carried me inside and up two flights of stairs before depositing me in my bed. He ran back downstairs and brought up a bucket, as by this stage I was vomiting non-stop all over myself and the floor. Attractive. The person who'd put me in a cab and returned me to the hostel was Harry. The models hadn't materialised and rather than spend his night picking up scantily clad women, he spent the entire night holding back my hair as I puked over the side of the bed. What a guy!

I woke in the morning to around three dozen missed calls from my husband, Joel, and realised I was at risk of missing my plane. Harry was asleep next to me, he hadn't left the entire night and was still wearing his new shirt and jeans; thankfully puke-free. I scrambled out of bed, shoved my belongings into my backpack and gently roused him to say goodbye. He smiled, bleary-eyed and fell back against the pillow. How would I ever repay him? I raced downstairs to where Billy Connolly was still manning the desk, and he called me a taxi.

"That was some powerful spewing you were doing last night, love," he said. "What the hell happened to you?"

"I have never been that sick in my life," I told him. "I have no idea what it was."

After he called the cab, he then asked me if I'd accepted any drinks from anyone that night. He seemed to suggest that he already knew the answer and was not surprised when I told him that Rick had given me a cocktail. As the taxi arrived he walked me out, wishing me the best for the rest of my travels and telling me to be safe. If it weren't for him and Harry that night, I don't like to think about what might have happened. It was the last time I'd ever accept a drink in a bar that I hadn't ordered myself. From a bottle. With a lid that had been removed in front of me. Never. Ever. Ever. Again.

6

Aquiles
(Cairns, Australia)

I had barely eased myself into the water, spun around, opened my book and read a whole sentence when I felt that all-too-familiar, visceral awareness of someone approaching. The hairs on the back of my neck rose, my shoulders stiffened and I willed the hair over my left ear to fall just low enough to cover my eye and hide my gaze from the stranger approaching me through the water. Before I knew it, there was an arm next to mine on the terracotta tiles and I let out a long and silent sigh. More of a scream, in hindsight. Here we go again. Just leave me alone. Leave me alone. *Leavemealoneleavemealoneleavemealone!*

Of course, as you've already read, I'm not an anti-social person and I'm not opposed to making new friends when I'm travelling. But when I travel for work, as was the case this time, I really prefer to keep to myself and enjoy a good book. I'm usually exhausted from a long day of meetings and talk-talk-talking to clients all day. So, when I get back to my hotel, I'll simply sit by the pool or outside on my room's standard-issue 3 x 3 balcony and watch the world go by. And so it was, on this warm night in steamy Cairns, that I was daydreaming of a luxury holiday in some far-flung subtropical paradise, with all the time in the world to enjoy the pool and my book; at least for the night.

'Hellooooooo,' the arm spoke. Or more likely, the person attached to the arm, but I cannot be sure, as I was doing my darndest to look grumpy, unapproachable and deeply interested in what I was reading. Meanwhile, I was having trouble even making it through the next sentence as I bristled at the unwelcome contact. I turned my head slowly (so as to convey more enthusiastically my disinterest in the conversation that was bound to burst forth).

"Hi," I said, with the least enthusiasm I could muster, while not coming across as a mannerless cow (manners at all times, if you please). My manners betrayed me though, as I couldn't help but include the slightest inflection in my reluctant greeting, which of course turned it into a 'Hi?' and warranted a follow-up answer.

"Whatcha reading?" came his reply, for it was a *he*, as it usually is. I had turned to face him, and in watching him speak, took in his appearance and made the one to two second assumption about his character, nationality, religion, sporting preferences and general douche-ish-ness (or lack thereof – rarely the case.) And oh, how I hoped I was wrong. The peaceful afternoon swim and reading session was at risk of being hijacked by a toothless, jobless bogan from the Back of Beyond. Perhaps I was a little premature – he actually had about six teeth (that I could count). A strong whiff of bourbon assaulted my nostrils, and his glassy-eyed glare betrayed to me that perhaps it was not his first drink of the afternoon. Or even his fifth.

I didn't even know how to attempt to answer the question. That stupid, mundane, *none-of-your-business-and-cant-you-tell-by-the-way-that-im-standing-against-the-wall-and-therefore-AWAY-FROM-YOU-that-I-don't-want-to-talk-to-you* question. How do I maintain a polite indignation? How do I answer just swiftly enough to not engage in further conversation, and yet not offend? How? How!

"A fucking book, moron," … is what I wanted to tell the idiot.

"Ahhh … a travel book" is what the quicker side of my brain instantly countered the bitchy part with, as I flipped the cover over to shoot him a glimpse at the artwork; a single, muddied hiking boot. Fairly explanatory, I thought. I gave a polite (but not fooling anyone) half-smile and gripped the book slightly closer to my chest.

"Oh yeah? And what does it entaaaail?"

He was breaking out the big guns now with words like 'entail'. He's clearly realised that chit chat about rum and coke or some such wasn't going to cut it with someone who knew how to read. I wasn't expecting this. I had to quickly compile a response before this guy stand-swimming beside me could mistake my silence for an invitation to fill the void. Or else, I could just high-tail it out of there immediately and end the conversation right then. Problematic. There was no way I could lift myself from the pool with any amount of grace at that depth, and the alternative was to wade, slowly and awkwardly to the steps at the other end. Crap!

"It's a travel book about a long hike." I decided to keep it brief, and introduce just a little hint of irritation into my voice. By this time, despite my unshakable need to remain polite, I had decided that this is not someone whose approval I required. Judging also by the fact that he appeared to be alone, and there were several other more approachable-looking bathers nearby, I came to the conclusion that should things turn ugly I would have support at hand.

"My name's Keith." He stuck out a wrinkled, tobacco-yellowed hand.

Of course it was. Reluctantly, I shook it and told him my name. Again, I added just the slightest hint more irritation to my voice and quickly snapped my hand back to grab my book. I hazarded a quick look back down to it, in an attempt to prove just how keen I was to get back to reading. You've had quite enough conversation now, Keith. Time for you to go, and me to get back to this damn book!

"You up here on holidays?"

For fuck's sake! Does this guy seriously have no understanding of the social cues for 'please fuck off' and 'I'm not interested'? Obviously not. Drunk Keith neither cared for nor understood these prompts. I was going to have to be forward in my next response, otherwise, I'd spend the entire rest of the night stuck in this infuriating conversation.

"I'm up here for work, actually." And before he could utter the 'what do you do for work?' that was resting on his lips as I looked straight at him, I steeled myself, and continued.

"And I've had a really long day. So I'm really just trying to get some reading done before I go up and do some more work." I tacked on a curt smile and tilted my head ever so slightly, to indicate an 'ok?' that I didn't have the balls to say. Politeness be damned!

"Oh, right. Well, it was nice to meet you. Have a *lovely* stay and enjoy your book," and with that he shook my hand again (cringe), shot me a meaningful, 'I'm glad you crossed my path on this beautiful night' look and swam away. If he had looked a little more like George Clooney and hadn't sprayed me with bourbon-tinged spittle from between his handful of teeth as he uttered his goodbyes, I would have felt sorry that I'd shooed him away. As it was, he didn't, he did, and I didn't.

I returned to my book (at last!) and couldn't make it more than a few lines through before I realised that I wasn't really reading it at all. I was skimming and thinking, my mind whirring and my senses all too alert for the possibility of more stealth-bogans. There was only one thing for it; a swim. I looked around, to ensure that Keith wasn't lurking in some shady corner of the pool, biding his time. To my delight, it seemed he'd left. Probably to go and chain smoke a few durries and father a few more illegitimate children. (*Alright, I realise that I'm being a bitch now.*) Dammit, I was just trying to relax!

I needed a few leisurely laps of the pool to ease my nerves. It was an incredible night. The sun had just started to lower behind the high-rises, the water was warm and still. Several elderly couples had entered the pool by now, and they gave me comfort with their placid smiles and slow strokes through the water. They weren't there to bother anybody. They certainly did not intend on starting any mundane conversations. They were there, as I was, to enjoy an early evening swim, in peace and quiet.

I made several laps around the lagoon-shaped pool and headed back for my book, where I'd left it sitting at the edge of the water. My nerves calmed, I reopened it with renewed vigour and greedily ate up the pages. I was sad that it was coming to an end; it was a great book. I tried to savour every word and make it last, but I couldn't help racing through it. I normally read slowly and quite deliberately, but this one was too good and I couldn't help myself. I was a binge-reader.

Rapidly reading away, the water now tranquil and drunkard-free, I was rather enjoying the idea of spending the next couple of hours here. I really didn't have anywhere to be, and I'd lied to Keith about having to head back to my room for more work. Why shouldn't I stay here until the hotel staff came and told me that swimming hours were over? I wasn't particularly hungry, and I could easily order a late supper from the room service menu if that changed at some point. It was decided then. I'd stay and read until either I'd finished my book, or the staff came to eject me. It was paradise, despite the slow creeping of mosquitoes from their daytime hidey-holes. Storks played in the mango trees swinging over the fence and I could hear dogs barking as their owners threw sticks along the beach. Joggers passed by on their evening ritual along the esplanade and guests emerged from their rooms to order drinks and dinner at the poolside bar.

It was a beautiful spot here; I'd have to remember it and have our corporate travel agent book it the next time I was visiting for work. I often begrudged having to go away for work to places like Cairns, Mackay, Cunnamulla or Toowoomba. But really, I could make the most of these trips with a pool like this and a good restaurant or two nearby (on company expenses, of course). The sort of loneliness I'd felt when travelling alone in South America didn't bother me so much when I was away for work. I could hide away in my room all night, order too much food and watch bad television if I so desired, and I wasn't disappointing anyone or 'wasting' precious downtime. If I felt social, I could step out into the hotel bar or venture further into town – if only to people-watch. Typically, a few dozen 'Drunk Keith's were lurking around, ready and willing to engage in banal conversation. For this reason, more often than not, I decided to stay within the confines of the hotel.

I did a few more laps of the pool for good measure, and sped through more chapters of my book. I hadn't been approached for any more distracting conversations, and merely encountered a few good-natured grins from my senior swimming companions as we passed like ships in the night. Or pool. Ships in the night in the pool.

It felt almost as though I was on holidays now; relaxing and with nowhere to be, at least until the morning. I was about to call it a night when I heard a 'hello!' from somewhere across the grass. I ignored it. Until again, slightly louder;

"Helloooo! Maggie!" I ignored it still. Oh no. Here he came. He'd found me and broken my reverie.

"Maggie! Helllooooo!" It was Aquiles.

Aquiles was a Chilean chap in his 60s or 70s that I'd met last night. As I'd stepped from the pool and headed to the bar to order myself an outrageous cocktail, an old gent arrived at the bar at the same time.

"After you," I'd offered, as the bartender looked to see who was next.

"No, no. Ladies first," he'd replied. I really wasn't in the mood to get into this back-and-forth, and so I smiled, thanked him and ordered.

"What are you reading there?" The most predictable and possibly annoying question I've ever encountered; here it was again. If I hadn't heard it from Aquiles on this first night, I may not have been so annoyed when interrupted by Keith on my next pool encounter. Well, not much less annoyed, given Keith's general demeanour. But I digress. Aquiles – as I would soon come to know – seemed harmless enough and so I answered his question. Again, I tried not to invite conversation, but I most certainly did not want to be rude to this old guy. He had a pleasant, grandfatherly look about him. He wore a cream fedora, cream safari-style shorts and a camera strapped around his neck, which jutted out over his round belly. He screamed 'European tourist' to me, and a tourist he was. Albeit, South American.

Despite my travels there only a year earlier, I had not picked up his accent at first. I had no ear for accents and could no more decipher Chilean from say, Italian as I could Irish from Scottish (having been to all of these countries did not help at all). I was hopeless with accents and still am.

"It's aaah …" I hadn't composed a response to this question yet, as I'd just started the book that day and hadn't a chance to think about how to define it to strangers yet.

"A book about a woman alone on a hike. It's non-fiction." He looked confused at the last phrase and so I clarified, "a true story?"

"Ah yes!" He gave a chuckle and I hoped the polite conversation would finish there. It was not to be.

"You should read my book," he chuckled again, barely audibly. I could have pretended not to hear him, he had spoken very softly. Once again, politeness got the better of me. For some reason, a woman alone at a bar carrying a book is an invitation to start a conversation. As is a woman alone with a book anywhere, for that matter. A woman alone at all actually seems to be a pretty good reason to strike up a conversation, come to think of it, and the book perhaps just provides the most obvious social lubricant and material with which to strike up such an exchange. I really needed to stop carrying my book around with me, it would seem.

"Oh, you are a writer are you?" Where the heck was this chat going to take me? There really is no polite way to remove yourself from this mess now, Maggie. Good work. Why is it that unlike 99 per cent of the population, I have the complete inability to smile awkwardly and walk away when someone is trying to engage me in discussion that I have no interest whatsoever in participating in? A moronic and twisted idea that somehow I'm being a prat if I don't respond, that's what. I've always had this feeling. I don't know where it came from. Perhaps my mother, who is an over-apologiser. She will apologise to someone for bumping into *her* in a supermarket, or stepping on *her* toe in a line at the shops. So do I, actually, and it's utterly ridiculous. Some anti-feminist, patriarchal brainwashing that a woman, a young woman, should always be courteous to a fault, and must always *be* at fault in any situation she's been unlucky enough to find herself in. I really must talk to my therapist about this. I really must *find* a therapist, come to think of it.

"Yes, yes. I write a book in Castilian. That is Spanish. I write a story of a lion and a lioness, Aquiles and Anita," he explained, with a thick (what I now realised) Chilean accent.

"Well, that's lovely. Is it based on a true story?" I was entangled, hook line and sinker now. I may as well make the most of it and engage in actual semi-interested conversation.

By now, we both had our drinks and were still standing at the bar, the bartender having disappeared to the other end to serve a new round of customers.

"Would you like to sit down with me so that we can talk some more?" he offered, in lieu of an answer to my question. He was clearly intent on making a night of it.

I had a freshly ordered cocktail in my hand and really couldn't come up with any acceptable excuse to deny him, and so I agreed and found us a seat nearby. So much for a cocktail, and then heading back for another lap or two, as I'd planned.

And so, we sat. I sipped slowly at my cocktail, trying not to wolf it down as I usually would. Not because I am an alcoholic, you see, but because I have the complete incapability to sip or chew slowly unless I consciously berate myself about it every few seconds and keep myself in check. I did not want to finish my drink so soon or I'd end up stuck in conversation with nothing in my hands. Also, I did not want to be drinking them too quickly and ordering more, ending up tipsy and trundling back to my room with a septuagenarian nipping at my heels. Aquiles sipped at his beer and told me about his book.

He'd written it after his wife had died five years ago, and a friend from Chile had suggested that he finally put pen to paper after years of procrastinating. And so, with very little else to occupy his time then, he did. He talked about wanting to publish it but not knowing how, and I offered him my limited advice on self-publishing and the resources he might use on the internet. He went on to tell me about his children and about how lonely he was, now that his wife was gone. He was travelling around Australia on his travel agent's advice (I'll bet!) and spending away his kids' inheritance by the sounds of it. He had a round-the-world trip booked next. Good on him, I thought. I told him that I wanted to write too, only that I never seemed to find the time. He would love to read my book one day, he told me.

My phone started to buzz beside me on the table, and Aquiles jumped as I opened it. It was Joel, my husband. He'd been trying to call for the last ten minutes and was probably getting quite worried. And no wonder; it was almost 9:00 pm! We'd been chatting for at least a couple of hours by now, and time had gotten away from me. I said my goodbyes to Aquiles, and he gripped my hand tightly.

"I am very glad to meet you, Maggie," he gushed "I probably never see you again. Thank you for talking with me, and I feel there is a reason you come into my life tonight." Ah jeez ...

I bade him goodnight and wished him the best with his travels, then rushed back up to my room to call Joel. Aquiles was off on a glass-bottomed boat trip to the reef the next day, and I was off south to Tully and Innisfail for more meetings, before heading back to the hotel again (no doubt, for more swimming and reading – and so it was).

When I'd ventured out to the pool again the next evening, book in hand, I'd had a slightly niggly feeling that I might see Aquiles waiting around by the pool for me. He was a lovely old guy, and I'd had a nice enough time talking to him. But, as happens with so many people I encounter, I found it hard to bring a close to the conversation and move along with my night without appearing rude or as though I wanted to rush off. Again, I seem to struggle with this in a way that other people do not. As I read my book and made lazy laps through the pool, I'd hoped that ridding myself of Keith would be the end of my awkward tête-à-tête encounters for that night.

My reverie broken, I raised my head once again from the pages of my book and there was Aquiles. Camera strap, cream pants and invisible *'I'm a tourist, how 'bout you?'* badge were leaning over the fence and waving in my direction. Oh boy!

"Hi Aquiles! How was your day today?" Here we go again, and again, and again ...

Grinning from ear to ear, he struggled for a moment with the fence mechanism and made his way over to me.

Standing a foot from the water's edge, while I stared up at him, he looked awkwardly down at me and began to tell me about his day.

"Grab a seat and drag it over," I suggested. Staring up at this angle gave the impression that I was glaring straight at his crotch and made me rather uncomfortable. He clumsily pulled a li-lo towards me and lowered his round frame down onto it, his white socks pulled up to his knees and gleaming in the low light. He stared at me for a moment, grinning. I hoped that remaining in the pool while we chatted would communicate my desire to keep the conversation short, as I was clearly busy read-swimming. He was still grinning with an air of senility.

"How was your day?" I repeated. "Did you go out in the glass-bottom boat?"

"Yes, yes. I just returned!"

"And, how was it?" I prompted. I could see this was not going to be as straight-forward and short an exchange as I'd hoped.

"Was good, it was good." He was still grinning.

"Did you see lots of fish?" Really, was I going to have to lead this entire chinwag?

"Yes, lots of fish. Lots of fish. Very good. Ah … Maggie, I hope that … would you, ahhh …" He stumbled over his words and I dreaded what kind of offer was coming, knowing that I wouldn't be able to muster the balls to refuse an invitation to a drink and more chatting at the bar. Honestly, what was wrong with me?

"Would you like to … ah … have a drink with me and we talk some more?" he finally stuttered. Oh crap!

It took me a few milliseconds to inwardly roll my eyes at myself and sort through my options.

"Ah, sure Aquiles. I just want to do a few more laps, and then I will meet you over there." Damn it!

"Ok, I go and get changed and come down in 20 minutes!" He responded, before grinning some more and eventually rising from his chair and dragging it back into place. I waved him off, and chastised myself for being so gutless once again. Now I would be stuck in the same situation, unless I was callous enough to leave now, make some excuse to the bartender to pass on, and head back to my room. All the while, hoping not to run into Aquiles as I left.

That's what I'll do, I thought. I'll run up to my room now, call down to the bar and pass on my apologies that I had work which I suddenly had to attend to. Yes, that was a good excuse. I paced the room and I undressed from my wet swimmers and sarong, and found new clothes to put on. As I untied my hair and tried to dry it, the minutes ticked past and I started to picture Aquiles grinning happily as he toddled down to the bar and looked around for me, then inevitably wandered over to the pool and wondered where on earth I could be. I pictured his face as the bartender saw him and passed on my message, and saw in my mind's eye, him sitting alone and downcast with a beer in his hand, having been stood up.

I couldn't do it. I couldn't do it to him. What was one drink and an hour or so out of my life to have a simple chat with a lonely man on his holiday, just looking for someone to relate to and to banter with? I'd never forgive myself now that I'd imagined his face.

I changed, headed back down to the bar and repeated the events of the night before almost line for line. Ah, Maggie. When will you ever grow a pair?

7

Rites of Passage in Bali

Since I can remember, I have had a healthy fear of... oh, just about everything. I don't know where or when this started; I don't recall any particularly hairy near-misses or brushes with death as a babe. Then again, there's a strong chance of blocking that kind of thing out, isn't there? Well anyway, none of my family reports any nightmare-inducing events that could have caused my fears; I suppose I was just a cautious child. I wasn't an adventurous sort at all back then. I never sped down hills in home-made go-karts. I had to stop at cracks in the pavement and slowly push my bike over them. I wouldn't rollerblade on even the slightest incline (for fear of breaking a wrist, of course!) Clearly, things have changed a little since then, and while I'm still scared of so many (soooo many) things, I've overcome enough of them to be able to travel as I have in the last few years. It did take time though, and it wasn't an easy lesson to learn.

It came as no surprise then, that I was petrified of flying before I'd ever stepped foot on a plane. I knew that flying in a giant metal bus in the sky was unnatural and that my body and mind wanted no part of it. Problem is, if you want to get to faraway places and see exciting things, taking a boat doesn't exactly fit into the schedule. (Let's be honest though, I'd probably be dead scared of ships as well, but I wouldn't know.)

I was a tee-totaller before I left for Bali in 2005, and had never even been on a plane before. (Oh, how times have changed!) My parents had offered to send me to the Sunshine Coast (three hours north of home) for a couple of weeks for my birthday and I thought I'd won the lottery. I'd just turned 22 and I was still young, poorly paid and under-travelled. A girl I worked with had mentioned that she was going to Bali a few months later, and that there was a huge special on flights. I had never even considered that the cost of flying to another country would be within my reach, and yet my Sunshine Coast holiday was not yet booked and paid for. I made a hasty phone call to Dad and asked if he'd mind putting that cash towards my flights instead of the Sunshine Coast trip. He agreed, and in fact thought it was a brilliant idea. Within the week, my flights were booked and I had sent off my passport application.

I asked my best mate and high school friend Cheri to come along with me and she jumped at the chance as keenly as I had. Heading to the airport that day, escorted by Cheri's family, we were more than a little excited. Eating Hungry Jacks in the food hall at the international terminal of Brisbane airport seemed exotic and overwhelmingly posh. We chatted away the time until the plane arrived and we were called forward to board. I remember thinking that there'd be some reason I would be refused entry to the flight. It was still so far out of my realm of experience to be flying in a giant metal bus to another part of the world where they spoke a different language and where armed guards carried machine guns at the airport.

Like an encounter with police, although innocent, you instantly scan your body and possessions for anything that might be construed as 'illegal', so was the feeling of getting through check-in, security and boarding for my first ever flight. I was 'packing it'. Needless to say, we made it through and found our seats on the enormous plane. We were seated near the front of the economy cabin, right in the middle section. I marvelled at the old-school ear phone jacks and dodgy big television on the wall in front of us. This was well before the ubiquitous wi-fi or smartphones, or even the monitor-in-the-back-of-the-headrest business of today. Though we still chatted away excitedly, I could feel a lump start to rise in my throat and my insides slowly start to turn to jelly. Not only had I never flown in a plane before, but my maiden voyage was set to be a five to six hour trip with an Asian airline I'd never heard of, to a country where recently Schappelle Corby had been arrested and sentenced to 20 years in prison for carrying kilos worth of marijuana.

We had forgone the proffered shrink-wrapping service for our luggage at the airport, sure that our padlocks would be enough to secure us from wanton drug-smuggling baggage handlers or corrupt officials. Considering my overly-cautious nature, which had only developed further since childhood, I am surprised that I was not more worried about these threats. Cheri must have calmed my fears somehow, although I'm not sure how she managed it. Kudos to her.

Before we knew it, the plane began to taxi down the runway and my heartrate began to rise. The noise was incredible, and despite having watched so much flight-related television over the years to the point of feeling as though I'd been and done this before, nothing prepared me for the sound and the shuddering that accompanied the takeoff. I screamed silent screams as Cheri dutifully held my hand. I'm sure she regretted it later; she had deep welts where I'd almost drawn blood due to the force of my fingernails against the inside of her palms. She didn't complain once, or let go of my hand. Bless that girl!

Finally we landed, but not before six hours or so in the air and at least 40 minutes of extreme turbulence. (My recollection of 'extreme turbulence' cannot be guaranteed to be accurate, as this was my first flight and I was possibly the victim of moderate to extreme flying anxiety.)

As I exited the plane and my feet touched the tarmac I strongly considered getting down on all fours and kissing the ground. Cheri gave me a look that said, *'Don't you dare! There are men carrying AK-47s and they will shoot you, YOU CRAZY PERSON!'* I acquiesced and chose to simply praise the flying gods, consider briefly converting from Atheism to Christianity, and thank 'The Academy' (wave to the crowd), my mother and the Holy Spaghetti Monster for this opportunity to NOT die in a fiery plane crash that day.

We made our way past the automatic weapons that were wearing tiny Balinese guards and into the terminal to collect our baggage and pass through customs. Another first for me, I shivered slightly and fidgeted as the official scrutinised my passport and looked at me disapprovingly.

"WhyyoucometoBali?" he blurted out. I didn't understand a word of it.

"Ah … Umm … excuse me?"

"WHY you come to BAAAAALI," he tried to slow things down for the moron he was talking to, and couldn't help adding a slight condescension to his tone. I was far too nervous to give him any lip.

"Ah. Oh right, um, we're here for a holiday. See, it's my first time! I have never been overseas before. We are staying for one week. Not far away. I promise I'm not smuggling any drugs or weapons or doing anything that would make you want to throw my ass in prison!" Ok, so I might not have actually uttered that last part out loud, but I was gibbering and he clearly wasn't interested in my plans. A simple 'holiday' would have sufficed. Eventually, he stamped my passport, shoved it back at me and let me go. Cheri, ever more worldly than me, breezed through without a drama. Then it was time to locate our bags, make it through the throng of people at the exit and locate a taxi to take us to the hotel. Without getting mugged, or murdered, or having our bags stolen, or getting ripped off by an unscrupulous taxi driver. Right!

No sooner had we picked up our bags from the carousel than we had little men buzzing around us and flittering over our bags while talking loudly and shouting quick commands at us. I had absolutely no idea what was going on. Soon our bags were being carried off by two of the small men towards the exit and out into the sweltering Balinese heat. All we could do was run after them, flailing our arms about and hoping we hadn't lost our bags forever. Those guys were quick! We ran through the exit and located the men, standing outside, with our bags still in tow. Turns out they were luggage carriers (unofficial) and wanted a small gratuity for the service. SERVICE? I was quickly becoming enraged. But I wasn't sure how things worked in this country and whether this was part and parcel. I didn't have any Balinese currency yet, and neither did Cheri. In the end, in order to get our bags back, I gave the guy an AUD$5 note and shooed them all away. We jumped into a cab, told the driver where we were headed and agreed on a fee beforehand. Pretty soon we arrived at the Bounty Hotel, Kuta.

Dripping with sweat in the tropical heat, we made our way to the reception and checked in to our rooms. Mercifully, the receptionist's English was immaculate and we didn't have any of the awkwardness I'd experienced at the airport with the word-vomit that occurred when I was nervous.

The entrance to the hotel was grand – all wood-carved, high temple-like ceilings and fresh, giant, exotic flowers. The 'Balinese' furniture back home did no justice to this place. It was epic. And extremely cheap. We made our way to our room, switched on the air conditioner (thank GOODNESS!) and changed – heading straight for the pool. As I mentioned, I wasn't a drinker before I had left for Bali. I didn't drink so much as an occasional wine spritzer. Nothing. Despite the hair-raising plane ride over, and the free beverage cart onboard, I hadn't succumbed. Drinking just didn't interest me. (Oh, if I knew me now ...)

Well, that lasted about half an hour. The swim-up pool bar was just too exotic not to take advantage of. Cheri had ordered a crush-style cocktail (lots of ice, some flavouring and barely any alcohol) and I took a sip when she offered. Damn, that was some tasty beverage! I ordered one for myself, and was handed a giant glass filled with *watermelon daiquiri.* As we needed simply to sign off our drinks to our room number, we stayed there into the wee hours, just adding drink after drink to our tab and getting pretty plastered. It was an excellent first night, and we'd thoroughly enjoyed ourselves. Smashed, we eventually crawled back to our room, which, conveniently, was only metres from the edge of the pool. After carefully brushing our teeth with bottled water and avoiding drinking the water in a fit of bliss while having a shower, we passed out in a boozy ecstasy until the morning.

I was woken by a large snarling noise that turned out to be my stomach. Oh dear! *Ohdearohdearohdear.* I rushed for the bathroom and spent several miserable minutes emptying the contents of my bowel, bladder and stomach at various intervals. Not pretty. This, I remembered, was why I didn't drink. After extricating myself from the bathroom, Cheri followed suit. We weren't feeling great, needless to say, and Cheri was sure it wasn't just your run-of-the-mill hangover. I couldn't imagine why. It took us hours to work out, while pondering our sickness over a meagre breakfast. The banquet was beautiful, but we couldn't bring ourselves to shove more than a few mouthfuls of toast and fruit into our mouths, simply for sustenance. It eventually dawned on us that despite our vigilance in teeth-brushing and shower-etiquette, we'd been drinking *ICE*-based cocktails all night. And I was pretty sure the hotel weren't making their ice cubes from bottled water. *Idiots!* We paid dearly that day, and didn't venture far from our air-conditioned suite. You live and learn, I suppose!

Before we'd left home, we'd asked our travel agent to organise a guide/driver through the hotel to take us around and see some of the more far-flung sights. On our next morning, he picked us up bright and early from the front desk. Ketut swaggered up through the lobby in jeans, boots, a rolled-up black business shirt and cowboy hat. He was much taller than any of the locals we'd come across yet. He had a warm smile and easy manner, and we liked him instantly. He was friendly and funny, and we greatly enjoyed being driven around by him in his Jeep that day. He took us up to the rice paddies an hour or so from the centre of Kuta where we admired the scenery and ate lunch at a mountaintop restaurant. Ketut warned us as we exited the Jeep not to touch any of the souvenirs shoved at us by the swarm of women standing in wait atop the mountain. 'You touch it, you have to pay for it,' he told us, and so we walked from the car with our hands firmly planted in our pockets and smiled benignly as we tried to extricate ourselves from the swarm.

Later, Ketut took us to a dressmaker, as I'd heard that having leather jackets made here in Bali could be extremely cheap. Naïve as I was, it wasn't hard to deduce that Ketut had taken us to see a family member of his for our leathery needs. They chatted away as I was fitted and measured up and eventually told that I could pick up my purchase in three days. After taking us back to our hotel, we offered Ketut a large tip; he'd spent at least six hours driving us around, after all. He refused point-blank to accept even a cent. I was so overcome that I leapt forward and gave him a huge hug. We'd miss our Balinese John Wayne. He chuckled, hugged me back and wished us well on the rest of our holiday. We waved him off as he drove away in a cloud of dust, exhaust fumes and swagger.

That night we hit the pool bar again, having galvanised our stomachs and overcome our Bali-belly (so much for being a non-drinker, eh?). We ate giant fresh seafood platters for the princely sum of about AUD$10. Come to think of it, the cheap food at least partly made up for what we were being charged for our drinks. By the end of the week we received a bill under our door for 4,000,000 rupee. Fuck Me! And I didn't drink? Senses dulled by booze, we happily drank away that night as though we hadn't a care in the world. We met a few other Aussies staying at the hotel and agreed to head out with them the next day to do some shopping.

Eight or more of us met up the next morning (all sporting sore heads but mercifully bug-free tummies) and sauntered out into the morning heat. Once outside the paradise of our hotel grounds, it was clear to see the poverty and dereliction that is downtown Kuta. Dirty children playing in gutters, women grabbing and haggling, trying to 'Braid your hair! Braid your hair!' and 'Do your nails! Do your nails!' It was chaotic and loud. I found it really overwhelming. We were constantly offered rides by the moped drivers, despite there being such a large group of us. I was really glad to have the company of the big Aussie blokes, who shooed away the hawkers and touts with much more efficacy than two lone girls could manage. We bought souvenirs and bartered effectively. We quickly discovered that there was a code among the stall-holders, who would signal to other savvy business owners about your bartering ability by giving you a different coloured bag. White means *'this guy's an idiot – you can take him for a ride! Three times the price for him!'* Whereas black meant *'has a clue what they're doing, you probably aren't going to feed your kids tonight.'* We did quite well and managed to gather a collection of black shopping bags by the end of the day. Although, we *were* given a mysterious black-and-white striped bag at one stage. We still have no idea what this meant, but liked to think it was *'yeah, they'll bargain with you but they're getting quite tired of this crap and just want that bucket hat, thanks'.*

Back at the hotel that night we had yet more swim-up pool bar drinks, along with the group of Aussie guys we'd met. One of them took quite a fancy to me, and we snuck a few sneaky pashes in a quiet corner of the pool. I could tell that Cheri was getting a bit agitated, but was too proud or polite to say anything. At home she was the party girl, always the life of the party and fiercely independent. She hated to be hung-onto by friends all night who wanted to hold hands to go to the bathroom. She liked to flit around and chat to everyone, and she loved to party hard. For this reason, I figured she wouldn't mind if I slunk away for a sneaky holiday shag with the young guy who'd taken a shine to me. He was a STAGGERING two to three years younger than me *(reooooowwwrrr, cougar!)*. In a drunken stumble, we made our way back to his room only to find it locked by his roommate who slept like the dead. For some reason (I blame booze) we thought it was perfectly acceptable to simply try each and every room door until we found one unlocked. We giggled, shut the door behind us and climbed into some poor soul's bed to do the deed and get up to a bit of monkey business (I'm not proud). No sooner had we crashed out, spent, on top of the sheets than there was a bang at the door and a rustle at the door handle. FUCK! I flung myself at the bathroom door and hid, while the rightful occupants burst into the room. I could hear a girl and two guys give my young accomplice an ear-bashing and then call out to me. There was nothing for it, as I couldn't hide in a stranger's bathroom all night. My clothes were scattered across the room and I faced the very real prospect of having to emerge, naked from the bathroom. Groping around in the dark I managed to find an altogether too-small towel and hastily wrap it around myself before taking a deep breath and emerging into the harsh florescent light. Mr Accomplice was still there, and motioned for me to head for the door. I bolted, and we slammed it behind us, leaving the three outraged and bemused occupants of the room behind. We chuckled and high-tailed it downstairs to find my room.

When we arrived, I could see Cheri's shape slumped over her bed through the curtains. She had the only key. Shit. I knocked quietly on the door. No answer. I knocked a little louder. Nothing. I banged now, running out of patience and quickly sobering up. She didn't as much as roll over. *Fuck it*, I thought. There was no way I was going to get into that room tonight. Either she was passed out and deep in dreamland, or else she was pissed at me for running off for a shag without her (wait – not that she'd want to come for that! You know what I mean). Probably the latter. And I deserved it. My shag buddy and I were stuck; he locked out of his room, and I out of mine. We could mosey on up to the front desk and disturb the night manager, but I was wearing nothing but a towel and he, his boxer shorts. Not to mention, why would he give either of us a spare key – we couldn't even prove who we were. There was probably a better solution to it, but in our inebriation and general foolhardiness we couldn't think of one. We camped out the front of his door until his room-mate finally awoke in the daylight hours and let us in. We crawled gratefully into his bed, and got a couple of hours sleep.

At a more reasonable hour, it was time for me to face Cheri; if she would let me in, that was. I decided to test the waters with an inter-room phone call. To my surprise she answered, and even agreed to let me in! Yahoo! I made my way down to our room and knocked lightly at the door. She opened it, with a disapproving look on her face. I apologised for leaving her alone the night before, and while she said she'd forgive me, she gave me just the slightest cold shoulder for the next couple of days. I deserved it.

8

Fuck Bolivia!

Back in South America: I'd made it out of Paraguay, albeit with a sore head and an important lesson learned. I landed at Santa Cruz airport in the late afternoon and made my way to my hostel. I'd booked for one night in a well-rated establishment, as I planned on heading out to Uyuni and the famous Bolivian Salt Flats the next day by bus. To my disappointment, the hostel was a few kilometres out of town and I couldn't see anywhere promising to find a meal for that night. I checked in and the receptionist gave me a list of shops and restaurants in the area with some vague directions. The roads were pock marked and maze-like, running in an increasing ring from the centre of 'town' and I didn't like my chances of finding any of the places listed while on my own and in the dark. Oh well, I thought, I can worry about that later. First – a shower. As the receptionist led me past the cool, grassy courtyard and back through the entrance gate I'd just come in, my spirits dimmed.

I'd found it a tad unnerving that the hostel was barely marked on the outside road and was surrounded by a large 7-foot retaining wall. I wasn't sure the cab had dropped me in the right spot for a moment, until seeing my confusion, he pointed out of his window to the small intercom on the wall. I had buzzed and waited briefly for an answer in Spanish which I wouldn't understand. The intercom made a crackling sound as the disembodied voice had clearly pressed the magic button and I pushed through the tall red gate. Inside the compound was an oasis of palms, clay tiles and large open doors leading into the main building. It was dark and cool inside and couldn't have felt more foreign from the surrounding sun-bleached, dusty streets. There were generous open-plan rooms branching off from the entrance hall and several large day beds, scattered with vast cushions. It looked more like an Indonesian retreat than a Bolivian hostel. There was a bank of computers against one wall which looked surprisingly modern, and I could just see the reflections of a pool bouncing against the walls of an outdoor area sporting yet more palms.

I was pleasantly surprised by the beauty of the cheap little refuge, and even hoped that I might come across some friendly fellow backpackers who would take pity on a lone female traveller and share their food for the night. This would save me having to brave the outside streets; possibly getting lost or kidnapped or mugged as I wandered aimlessly in search of sustenance. As I followed the receptionist out of the main building and across the street, my hopes started to fade. She opened another unmarked gate and led me through a dirty and unattractive stone courtyard which was surrounded by four yellow doors. To the back of this courtyard was my room, and she handed me a key, pointed to the shower block which was supposedly behind another of the yellow doors and left me there to my own devices.

I hauled my backpack into my room and stared into the darkness for a few moments while my eyes adjusted. The room was large and cool, but sparsely decorated with a double bed and a single table pressed against the window. After a few minutes of searching around, I found the light switch and busied myself unpacking my bag in search of clothes that were long overdue for a wash. Unpacking was my go-to activity for relaxing and unwinding and gathering my thoughts in new surroundings. Moving every few days to a new hostel was off-putting and I found that the simple task of removing items from my backpack and placing them around the room made each room feel a little more mine and just a tiny bit less like it belonged to the hundreds of other people who'd occupied it before me.

I had my dirty clothes in a vac-sealed bag in order to not pollute the rest of my luggage with their stench. Having unloaded the contents of my pack and neatly organised my small collection of toiletries across the table, I picked up the vac-bag and headed across the courtyard to find the shower block. Disconcertingly, the lock on the door to the only shower was pretty suspect and barely made a 'click' as I slid it across into place. It jiggled loosely on its screws and I wondered if it had been forced open from the outside at one point. Gulp!

Although it was late afternoon by this stage, it was still bright and sunny in the courtyard outside and so I tried to put all nasty thoughts out of my mind. I busied myself washing my gnarled hair and my array of dirty laundry in the cold shower. I would soon discover that hot (or even warm) water was almost non-existent in Bolivia, as were wi-fi and many other things I'd come to take for granted in my travels. Still, a cold shower didn't bother me as much as the sparks and buzzing that would occasionally fly from the electric (and completely redundant) heating unit attached to the showerhead. I decided not to spend too long under the water, and hurriedly finished up, heading back to my room. I used yet another threadbare towel to dry myself (I wonder if there are any other kind in South America?) and hung it over the bed frame as there was nowhere else to put it. Then I methodically hung each of my wet items across the frame as well, and several of them up over the curtain rod when I ran out of space. Though it was hot and dry outside, I didn't like my chances of these drying overnight as the nights in Bolivia were cool. I didn't feel safe leaving the window cracked to allow a flow of air through my room, and so I hoped that the fan would suffice; lest have to repack them wet.

All of the settling-in tasks complete, I sat for a while on my bed and contemplated my dinner options. As I'd had good luck with meeting friendly travellers in other hostels, I decided to try my luck in the common area beside the pool. I went for a walk across the road and into the main compound, where the receptionist was nowhere to be found. I ventured through the rooms and out into the pool area. It was cool and tranquil in this little oasis, although the surrounds of concrete and tiles meant no breeze could pass through the palms that edged the courtyard. There was nobody around, and although I would normally have sat with a book and read until someone came along, my stomach betrayed me. It had been a long day already and I hadn't eaten since that morning. There was nothing for it but to go searching for a 'corner store' which I'd hoped would appear mere blocks from my door and serve me up some beans and rice, or even an empanada. I consulted the map I'd been given upon check-in and it seemed to suggest (albeit in Spanish) that there were several stores and restaurants around. There was no scale listed on the diagram and so I had very little idea of how far away these places were.

I headed out without much of a plan, as I was sure I'd stumble upon something. I walked for two blocks before coming to a sharp curve in the road and a park of sorts. Two youths walked through the park, thankfully not in my direction. However, I decided that navigating a strange stretch of grass and trees by myself would not be clever. It was beginning to get dark and I was starting to lose my nerve. Dogs barked behind fences and out of sight as I followed the curve in the road. There were very few people around, and not a single car parked on the street. I wasn't sure whether to be grateful or wary of the apparent quiet in the neighbourhood. Just when I was thinking that I'd have to turn back, dinnerless, I saw a dim light in the distance. My spirits rallied slightly and I followed the road for another two blocks before coming upon what looked like a small store-cum-garage-cum-slumhouse. There were two men sitting on creaky plastic chairs outside who eyed me suspiciously, yet didn't utter a word. I was beginning to get a *House of a Thousand Corpses* vibe, but my grumbling stomach won out and I headed inside. A short, round woman entered from a backroom to stand behind the counter. She didn't offer me any help or greet me in Spanish, and I suspect she'd come to ensure I didn't steal anything. I uttered a hopeful *'empanadas?'* to which she shook her head. I mimed putting a large, juicy burger to my mouth and chewing. She looked puzzled, and then pointed to a stack of burger buns behind me. Ok, I thought, this is a start, but how the heck was I going to cook my own burgers? Or did she just expect me to eat the buns? I made some more excellent miming gestures to signify a burger patty or sausage – but no joy. She was starting to think I was a crazy person. I turned and browsed the store to look at my other options. Everything was packaged and indecipherable. There were batteries, cans of drink, packets of gum, and fishing wire. What exactly that was for, I couldn't say; there was no water in the area which was suggestive of fishing. Finally, I settled on what looked like a packet of what I assumed were savoury biscuits, paid and left, deflated. An exciting dinner of plain biscuits was ahead of me.

It was now properly dark outside and I was beginning to get a little more fearful, wondering whether I'd find my way back to the hostel – and in one piece. I made a phone call to Joel in order to feel a little less alone, but the line was crackly and it just made me feel homesick and sad. I tried not to inflect fear in my voice as I said a quick goodbye and then consulted my map again. I hadn't really taken any turns, as I'd followed the curving road around until I'd come upon the store, but everything looked different in the dark. More dogs barked which set off a chain reaction of howls into the distance and I wondered whether they were signalling their big, bad owners that a lone and lost idiot was approaching. I began to walk a little quicker as I heard faint footsteps down side streets and caught glimpses of a disappearing ankle in the shadows now and then. I pulled my hotel key out of my pocket and held it tightly, ready to use as a weapon should anyone truly scary decide to try their luck with this stupid, stray girl.

Just as the dogs quietened down and the silence became eerie and almost unbearable, the lights of the hostel came into view; faint yet welcoming. Huge relief swept over me as I turned the key into my side of the compound and burst through the door into my room. I collapsed onto the bed in exhaustion, my stomach barely registering my hunger anymore. I pushed aside the packet of biscuits and fell into the kind of sleep that a fugitive must feel when he's found a dry place to sleep and avoided the search-lights for another night. That night I dreamed I was in the desert, running from an unknown beast in the semi-darkness. I came across a train track and ran until a cargo train approached from behind, its huge headlights lighting up the road in front of me and turning my shadows into long, spindly caricatures of my legs and arms. I jumped into one of the carriages as the train passed and as I was congratulating myself on my skills in train-hopping, a figure loomed out of the corner and bared it's stained, yellow fangs.

I woke with a start, it was daylight. I had made it through my first night in Bolivia and it was time to head to the train station. I had read in my online *Lonely Planet* wanderings that you could not buy bus tickets in Santa Cruz online, or even a day in advance. And so, you had to arrive on the day you wanted to travel and barter with the myriad of bus company touts to find the best price to your destination. No problem, I thought!

When my taxi dropped me off outside the transport hub, I thought he was having a laugh. A great expanse of dust and crumbling concrete stretched out to the right and what appeared to be a shanty town built up around decrepit, once-glorious hotels spread out to the left. The driver pointed to the right and I pulled my pack from the boot, wary and unsure about the day ahead. I could see people slowly trickling into the building. It was only 7:00 am. I had no idea what time the buses would be leaving or, in fact, how long it would take to get to Uyuni. Not sure what to expect, I hesitated as I entered the giant concrete structure and waited for my eyes to adjust in the relative darkness. Once everything came into focus, I couldn't help but stop in shock. There were dozens and dozens of shop fronts lit up with different company logos, pictures of buses, and names of various destinations. It appeared they hadn't been long open, as staff still pulled up the occasional roller door and blearily set up for the day. It wasn't long before I began to be approached by men offering their services, shouting destinations at me as though I was likely to choose one on the spot. *'Uyuni?'* I kept asking, to which many shook their heads and looked bewildered. My Spanish was still terrible and I wasn't even sure that I was pronouncing it correctly. I passed signs in Spanish that I couldn't decipher, and after several more head shakes and puzzled glances I was beginning to wonder what on earth I'd got myself into. I could be here for days, trying to figure this out.

I'd optimistically booked myself a night in the famous Salt Hotel outside of the town of Uyuni, in anticipation that it would take me roughly 24 hours to get there by bus. I needed to get on one of these damn buses today, and the sooner the better. I was approached by yet another tout, who sauntered towards me with a large grin on his face and I'm sure he thought, *Ah! A nice clueless gringo for me to rip off!*

"Where you going, lady?" he asked, in English. I could have cried with relief, and I'm sure it showed on my face. Clearly this guy had the edge, as his counterparts spoke barely a word of English; much like the rest of South America so far.

"Ahhh … Uyuni? Salt Flats?" I proffered, hopefully. I couldn't handle one more head shake and rejection.

"Yes, si, si! Uyuni! This way!" He gestured towards his little green shop front and the tiny office behind it. I hadn't noticed any offices at the other windows, and as he led me inside I wasn't sure whether to feel at ease or on edge. He offered me a chair at his desk as he squeezed in behind it and began to tap away on his ancient computer.

"Um, how long is it to get to Uyuni?" I asked, as he pulled out a receipt book and a calculator.

He thought for a moment, looking back towards the computer screen which was turned away so that I could not make out what it displayed.

"Twenty-three hours," he said. "Nice bus, nice bus for you!"

"Full *Kama* bus?" I gestured the lie-down seats and mimed the international symbol for sleep: two hands folded under my tilted head, my eyes closed.

"Si, si – nice bus for you! *Kama* bus!" I was instantly relieved again, and he could see it on my face. Actually, I'm certain he saw dollar signs atop my shoulders rather than a head. He began to hand write me a receipt and punched out some numbers onto the calculator, which he then showed to me, by way of a quote. It came to around USD$50 and I thought, although this seemed steep, it was nothing to me for a 23-hour bus journey and was still much cheaper than a flight. I eagerly handed over the cash, and was only a tiny bit confused when the printer spat out what looked like a bus ticket and he folded it and put it into his wallet – along with my cash. He handed me the handwritten receipt on which he'd scrawled the destination and the time of departure. He'd not written down the price, but he had included a seat number. It appeared that I had a window seat. Excellent!

I wasn't quite so enthusiastic when I realised that the bus was not due to leave until 5:00 pm. It was still only 8:00 am and so I had quite a bit of waiting around to do. No problem, I thought, I could simply go and find some food and a quiet place to sit and read my book. This was a holiday after all, and I shouldn't be opposed to having some downtime. I left the shop, was assured that I merely had to return here one hour before my departure time and I made my way back out through all of the touts and other shop fronts towards the far end of the building. I had a smug air of accomplishment about me, as I made my way through the now-thick sea of people. As more men shouted destinations at me and bared their greasy smiles, I shooed them away with a half-smile and a casual manner that said, *I'm sorted buddy; it's not your lucky day*. I always feel at ease before catching a flight or a train when I have time to spare. I'd much rather arrive early and have hours of relaxing ahead of me, in clear view of the platform I need to be on and without the worries of traffic congestion, overzealous security checks and mad rushes to the gate. I managed to find the food hall that was located on a second level in the giant concrete hanger-style structure and I perused the outlets slowly, so as to soak up more of my time and more importantly, make sure I didn't decide too hastily on what to eat; as too often happens to me. I get all in a fluster in a new place which I am not sure how to navigate. Even in a shopping mall at home, I'll find myself in a tizz and confused, and end up buying whatever just barely suits what I need in the very first shop I can find it in, just so that I can leave and not spend all of my time looking around like I have no idea where I am or what I am doing.

I settled on a large fast-food style restaurant with hundreds of plastic chairs and the smell of roast meat emanating. I could not understand a single thing on the menu except for the word 'carne' (simply, meat) and so I made some mutterings to the waitress behind the counter and did some pointing. The pictures were nondescript, faded and seemed to show a variety of different coloured slop on plates with rice or chips. I would be happy with either the rice or the chips and so I was not too concerned about what would eventually present itself to me. I paid and took a seat, watching other diners file into the restaurant and order much more succinctly and confidently than I had. Before long, my meal was placed in front of me and I couldn't for the life of me tell you what it was.

There did appear to be chips somewhere hidden under a pile of yellowish mush (maybe curry?) and what I suppose was meant to be a salad; droopy and wilted lettuce leaves and some kind of dressing. There was no rice, and I was a little disappointed at this although I ate it all greedily and mopped up my plate with the last of the chips.

I took another look at my watch and groaned when I realised it was still only 8:45 am. I picked up my leather satchel (the man who'd sold me my ticket took my pack and strapped a ticket with a number on it, telling me that it would be loaded onto the bus for me), found a seat at the back of the restaurant and sat there for the next several hours.

Finally, 3:30 pm rolled around and I thought it was a good time to head back down to the terminal and begin waiting for the bus to arrive. Still standing outside his office, the man who'd sold me my ticket was waiting and chatting to some friends who all appeared to work for one of the bus companies. He welcomed me over with another greasy grin and introduced me to the other men. One of them offered me a seat, and before taking it I tapped my watch and indicated that it was soon time for my bus to arrive.

"Ah, is not come until 6:00 pm. You sit here," greasy man told me. What?! There was a delay on my bus, it seemed. I still had another two and a half hours to wait. Great! Oh well, they all seemed friendly enough and so I took a seat and got out my Spanish phrasebook. Before long, another three men had come to join the conversation and they all chatted away, shooting sideways glances at me and pointing every now and again. When I'd catch one of the men's eyes he would beam a wide grin at me, usually with no more than half a dozen teeth to his name. I tried not to catch their eyes too often though, for occasionally one would linger a little too long or move in closer for a better look at the white girl.

I found that I could blend in easily enough in most places here, with my long dark hair and slightest hint of a tan. However, my eyes gave me away, and so I tried to wear sunglasses when I could. Without fail, on each occasion that I had to take them off and speak to somebody they would gasp and utter something along the lines of, '*Oh! Your eyes, so blue! Amazing!*' before dragging me by the hand to introduce me to someone else who had apparently never seen a blue-eyed woman before. Needless to say, eventually one of the men noticed and it became the instant topic of conversation for the whole group. Mr Greasy translated a sentence for me every now and then. It seemed that most of them wanted to know if I was married (yes), what I was doing out here alone (on a holiday) and why on earth my husband would let me come here alone (none of your damn business). As I had to explain this over and over again, I tried to use my phrasebook to answer their questions and then turn the conversation in a different direction. As I leaned forward to take a small bun offered to me by one of the men, my shirt slipped ever so slightly up from my belt and exposed my tattooed side. Mr Greasy was watching intently and then gasped as he noticed the tattoo.

"Ah! Tattoo!" he shouted, beaming. He was clearly pleased and I could tell that perhaps it boosted my street cred a little, and I grinned back nonchalantly, mouthing, 'Yep, sure is.'

"Come, you come with me!" He pointed inside to his office and I assumed that it was time to head to my terminal. Once inside, and away from the others he pointed towards my side and asked for me to show him my tattoo. Little alarm bells started to go off in my mind, and I knew that this was not the kind of person I wanted to be stuck in a room with, baring my flesh. He had been nothing but friendly and jovial, however, and I still needed to make sure that he sent my bag to the right bus. I thought it was surely harmless, and I lifted my shirt again just a little so that he could see it. He grinned a sickly grin and lurched forward to touch it. I moved back a little, just out of his reach and shook my head at him as if to say, 'ok, you've had your fun but that's far enough.' He looked back up at me and straightened a little to lighten the mood. He laughed heartily and shook his hand at me as if to say, 'don't worry girl, I'm just curious'. I laughed back and then as I was about to lower my shirt, he lunged forward again and tried to shove his hand down the side of my jeans. I gasped, and smacked his hand away, unsure as to what the appropriate action should be. There were a lot of people around and I was in no great danger. However, there were several of his mates outside who could easily barricade me in here in this tiny office, if it took their fancy. I quickly pulled my shirt back down and stepped away. I stood firmly, planted my feet a shoulder width apart and crossed my arms, in an attempt to appear as strong and capable as possible. I laughed, although with a hint of gruffness to my voice and said, 'Ok, ok. That's enough!'

He laughed back and shrugged his shoulders, heading back out of the office and into the waiting area. I sighed and relaxed. What an IDIOT, I thought to myself. I cannot afford to be getting myself into these kind of situations and be so naïve! I'd had enough of Mr Greasy and his mates and I wanted to get onto my bus. I burst through the back door of his office, which lead out onto the waiting platform where there were hundreds of people gathered. Buses were pulling in and out of the bays, and luggage was being thrown hither and thither. I noticed a young couple waiting patiently at my terminal and I approached them, hoping against hope that they'd speak English.

"Ah, hallo. Habla Englais?"

"Yes, hello, we speak English!" the young guy offered, smiling with what looked like a full set of teeth. I was instantly comforted.

"This is my girlfriend Maria, she is from Spain. And I am Bolivian, my name is Enrique." They were warm and welcoming. We chatted about what they were up to, and it turns out that Maria was visiting from Spain and was about to head out for a few days on her own while Enrique headed back to work. See? I thought, she's on her own in a foreign country and she looks capable! Never mind that she speaks perfect Spanish, and therefore is leaps and bounds ahead of me!

"Do you have a ticket, Maria? Do you mind if I see it?" I was well and truly over the honeymoon phase with Mr Greasy and was beginning to wonder whether my handwritten receipt would really pass for a ticket. Maria happily pulled out her ticket which was quite clearly NOT handwritten. She was waiting for the same bus that I was, but her destination was completely different. Fuck!

"Do you think the bus is stopping here?" I pointed to her ticket and the destination "and then continuing on to Uyuni?"

She shook her head, as they both took a look at my dodgy receipt. They weren't sure, but they didn't seem convinced. I was starting to get more than a little worried and by now it was after 6:00 pm. I thanked Maria and Enrique and marched back through the back door to the office. I found Mr Greasy sitting outside and I walked purposefully up to him, brandishing my useless piece of paper.

"My ticket!" I almost shouted '*Now!*'

"Ok, ok, no worries," he said. He pulled his wallet from his back pocket and produced the ticket which had been printed from the computer earlier. He handed it over to me and I took a quick look at it, immediately knowing that something was still not right. He'd crossed out the printed destination and written in black marker '*Uyuni*' over the top of it. He'd also crossed out the price I'd paid (or should have paid) so that I couldn't read it. Otherwise, it looked identical to Maria's and so I took it and headed back out the door just as a bus pulled into the bay.

Maria and Enrique had disappeared into the throng of people and I caught a quick glimpse of my bag being herded with a hundred others into the luggage compartment.

Big, shiny buses pulled up in the adjacent termi-nals, and I could make out their gleaming, comfortable leather seats through the tinted windows. Full Kama buses have 180-degree, fold down seats for optimum sleeping comfort. They have at least one onboard toilet and serve three meals a day. If you're really lucky, you also get a TV set which plays awful Spanish movies or over-dubbed Hollywood flicks. We'd caught one of these buses from Buenos Aires to Iguazu, and I had slept peacefully and played card games the whole way.

What had pulled up in our terminal was NOT one of these buses. It looked like something straight out of *Romancing the Stone*. Crusted yellow paint, creaking bi-fold doors and row upon row of old school bus bench-style seating. No leather. No fold-back 180-degree seats. No meals. No toilet. For 23 hours.

I was jostled on board with the rest of the passengers, and caught sight of Enrique waving goodbye to Maria. He gave me a wave and shouted, 'good luck!' over the hubbub of the swarming passengers. I was in shock as I worked my way to the back of the bus and eventually found my seat. It was indeed a window seat. If nothing else, Mr Greasy hadn't lied about that. As I sat down in abject terror at the ride ahead of me, a large Bolivian woman crammed herself in beside me with what I'm fairly sure was a sack of live chickens on her lap. The very worst thing about travelling alone is not having a partner in crime to share your thoughts or apprehensions with. It is a times like these that it is advantageous to be able to turn to the person next to you and say, 'Am I just being a princess because I don't want to sit on a bus with no toilet for 23 hours – OR, is this fucking bullshit?'

I sat there weighing up in my mind the seriousness of the situation. Could I really make it that long in this awful seat, with a metal bar pinned against my back and with no toilet for 23 hours? How did I fancy that large Bolivian woman next to me falling asleep on my shoulder? (Or for that matter, how would she feel about finding this pudgy white girl drooling over her in the middle of the night?) Not to mention the fact that clearly most of the other passengers, including my neighbour, had never heard of deodorant and were blissfully unaware of its miracles in stink prevention. Would this just be another story that I could add to my tales of South America? Remember that time the crazy greasy creep sold me a dodgy ticket on a dilapidated 1950s school bus with no toilet and I sat next to a bag of chickens for 23 hours? What a hoot!

As I stared out the window like a prisoner on a transport bus to Azkaban, I watched another gleaming full Kama bus pull out beside us, its passengers settling into their reclining seats, blankets already pulled up tight around their chins and dozy, comfortable smiles on their faces. FUCK IT, I thought. FUCK. THIS. SHIT.

I jumped up and out of my seat and made my way over the woman and her chickens. Down the aisle, I was not careful as I stepped on toes and bags and probably a few fingers as a red mist of rage came over me. I was getting off this DAMN bus before it pulled out of the terminal and it was too late. I burst through the half-closed doors and out onto the platform below. A luggage clerk looked at me, bemused. I shouted that I wanted my bag and gestured towards the compartment he'd only moments ago finished filling. He could not have been more than 15 years old. He followed my gaze to the undercarriage and then looked back to me, utterly confused. I could see the last of the passengers were making their way to their seats and I had little time.

As bad as my Spanish is, it seems that a woman screaming furiously, 'GET MY FUCKING BAG OUT, NOW!' and madly gesticulating at the baggage compartment while waving around her luggage tag number is fairly universally understood. And so, reluctantly, the clerk climbed under the bus and began to pull bag after bag out and offered each of them to me. It seemed as though he was happy to just give me any bag I liked, simply to see the back of me as quickly as possible. I shouted some more and pointed further into the pile until eventually out came my backpack. He stood silently agape as I took it from him and hoisted it to my back. The red mist still hung low over my mind's eye and I marched purposefully back into that Godforsaken office once again. No more Mrs Nice Girl – no more shyness, no more manners. Mr Greasy was nowhere to be seen, and so, with tears held back, I strode out into the throng of people inside, looking for another ticket vendor. I hadn't made it more than a few feet before I heard a familiar voice and was greeted by that sickening grin once again.

"Maggie! You miss your bus?" He beamed at me. I'm sure he thought that this was just another chance to sell me an overpriced ticket on another wretched, stinking bus and so he grabbed my arm jovially to lead me back towards his office. I yanked my arm away from him and let loose a barrage of language that made heads turn from every direction. I only managed to hold back the tears by the sheer force of my screams and foul language. Mr Greasy cowered, shrinking to half his size as he took my hurled insults like bullets and winced at each strike. I followed as he pitifully crept back towards his office, wounded and belittled in front of prospective clients and what I suspect were also terminal officials. Once inside I continued my assault, hurling 'FUCKS' like projectiles and hoping to injure him further with each and every one. I was done with being taken advantage of, and I was having none of it! As he cringed and trembled, he managed to pull his wallet out from his pocket once again. This time, he offered me a solid lump of cash that rested within, the entire contents of his wallet; my full payment. I snatched it from him, hurled a few more invectives his way and stormed from the office, tears now finally beginning to stream defiantly down my cheeks and into my hair. I sucked them back, wiped my face with the back of my sleeve and surged forward away from Mr Greasy and his shocked entourage.

"Maggie!" I heard a shout and looked up, not having the faintest idea of who was now trying to get my attention. It was Enrique. His head bobbed in and out of the crowd until he reached me. I showed him my refunded cash and he whistled, long and low.

"Maggie," he said, "You just beat a Bolivian over money! That never EVER happens!" He grinned and patted me on the shoulder, in awe and disbelief. As he headed away in the other direction after another wish of 'good luck', I continued down the strip with new zeal. I could do this. I could do this. I could do this.

I found another office who were still selling tickets and whom above blazed the logo I'd seen on the mythical Kama buses I'd seen pull up only feet from my horror bus. I approached the desk and noticed that the vendor here had his computer screens turned towards the public, making it clear which seats and which buses were available; no nonsense. Thank GOODNESS! I sighed audibly as I made eye contact with the man behind the counter.

"English?" I asked. He shook his head and said, 'a little'. Better than nothing, I thought. He could clearly see that I'd been through an ordeal, but whether he'd heard my torrent of vitriol moments ago, I couldn't say. I asked, 'Full Kama, Uyuni?' to which he laughed, and nodded. The look in his eye told me that yes, he had heard, and yes, he could help me. I sighed again and laughed back. He drew me up towards the counter and showed me the diagram of the full Kama bus, with UYUNI clearly typed across the top of the screen. He sold me a ticket for a bus that was leaving at 9:00 pm, still another hour and a half away. The ticket cost less than a fifth of what Mr Greasy had charged me.

Relieved, exhausted and thoroughly (although perhaps unfairly) sick of Bolivia, I wandered the building until I found an internet café. Just for laughs, I decided to look up flights to Uyuni online. I'd searched for them days earlier and decided that they were too expensive, at around USD$150. I had been looking forward to a bus ride through central Bolivia and from the comfort of my leather seat, expected to get a taste for the landscape from an air-conditioned and padded, safe distance. The shine had worn off this vision somewhat over the last few hours, and before I knew it I'd entered my credit card details on the airline's website for a flight out of this hell hole at 10:00 am the next morning. I'd been waiting at this bus terminal now for 12 hours, and my flight the next day was due to take merely two 45-minute legs (stopping at La Paz) to reach my destination. I couldn't help but laugh at the situation I'd put myself in that day. I scrolled the booking. com website and found the most expensive and luxurious looking hotel in town, at USD\$120 and made my way finally back out to the street. It was dark now, and cooler. Throwing away my new bus ticket, I wandered down the road until I found a taxi passing and hailed it over.

I checked in at reception and made my way up to my room. I passed down the corridor lined with large, sturdy oak doors, each glazed and beautiful and expensive. When I found my door, and turned my key I almost wept with joy at what I found inside. A giant living room and kitchen was gently lit by lamps already switched on and waiting for me. I made my way through to the bedroom and my heart skipped a beat at the king-sized bed and plush, feather pillows. As if I could have been any more indulged and amazed, I choked a little on my intake of breath as I rounded the corner into the ensuite. Before me lay a huge bathtub and marble vanity unit, sheathed in more dark, stained oak. I stripped off and stood in ecstasy below the shower. I scalded my skin unrepentantly with the hottest water that the pipes could muster and washed away the trials and odour of the day. For good measure, once I was scrubbed and clean and pink with heat, I ran the bath. I poured hotel shampoo into it and swished it around with my feet until large bubbles formed and enveloped me softly. I drifted in and out of sleep, as the bubbles began to slink away and the water began to cool. I drained the bath and looked down at my now soft and gleaming skin, feeling refreshed and dozy all at once. Then I ran another shower, just for good measure. Who knows when I'd have hot water again?

9

Uyuni or Bust

The next morning, bright and early, I headed back in my taxi past the now infamous Bolivian Bus Depot and headed once again for Santa Cruz airport. Feeling thoroughly clean for the first time in weeks, I knew I'd soon be missing the hot shower and bathtub I'd enjoyed last night. I'd slept deeply and contentedly in the king-sized bed and built a fort of pillows to surround and protect me from the dangerous world outside. As I sped along in the back seat of the taxi over potholed, chaotic roads, I wondered what lay ahead in Uyuni. I had half a mind to just catch the first available flight out of Bolivia and say goodbye to the country before it would snare me in its grasp again and this time, not let me off so easily. I was planning to head to Peru next and visit the ancient city of Machu Picchu. I could scarcely afford the cost of another plane ticket, simply to throw the one I'd already bought away. I thought long and hard as the streets of Santa Cruz flew by. Eventually, before finally entering the international terminal of the airport,

I regained my sense of adventure and threw caution to the wind. I headed instead for the domestic terminal and boarded my flight to Uyuni.

Sitting in the small, but surprisingly modern aircraft, I felt somewhat at ease. The plane didn't look as though it was missing any vital components and the crew appeared to be professional and most importantly, unfazed by our impending departure. I pushed hysteria and fantasies of third-world, fiery plane crashes to the back of my mind and ordered a cup of coca tea. Before long we were in the air and I waved a secret goodbye to the Godforsaken city below – hopefully for the last time!

The flight time was a breezy half-hour to the city of La Paz, with a four-hour layover and then another 45 minutes to Uyuni. The first leg to La Paz was uneventful and I spent my four-hour layover inside the airport, getting an hour long and serene 'altitude massage', and sitting in a café drinking tea and orange juice, and eating pastries. The airport was a modern oasis after all I'd experienced in Bolivia so far.

I peered out of my porthole window on the final leg, and I could see the famous salt flats of Uyuni come into view. Vast expanses of white plains spread out before me, seemingly all the way to the horizon. The sun morphed from a golden, high afternoon orange to deep sunset red as we flew towards the tiny city perched among the flats. Shades of deep purple and pastel pink splashed across the sky and I sat back, content. I was feeling relaxed and unhurried on this day of short flights and squeaky-clean airport living and was finally beginning to forgive Bolivia for its less than warm welcome. The flats spread out before me at unbelievable distances and just as I began to make out scattered buildings below, something strange happened, and I was pulled from my reverie. We were turning around. Ok, I thought, no big deal. Perhaps we need to approach from the other direction? It happens often at home. But as we turned, the pilot didn't make a full circle and the village below grew smaller until finally it was out of sight again. Not a peep from anyone else sitting nearby, I began to stress a little. What the hell was going on? Was I missing something?

Eventually, the pilot came over the speakers in the cabin announcing something in Spanish, of which I understood little, and then finally in broken and heavily accented English; of which I understood only a few words. Among them were 'turning back' and 'dust storm'. Fuck! Fuck you, fucking Bolivia! Seriously? A 45-minute flight, and you didn't think to call ahead and check that the coast was clear? Are you telling me that in the last half-hour or so, a dust storm of such strength as to throttle an aircraft has appeared out of the sky and NOBODY KNEW ABOUT IT BEFORE NOW? WHAT THE *FUCKING* FUCK BOLIVIA!

My mini-meltdown over, I soothed myself with deep breaths and assurances that this must happen all the time, and surely we'd circle back once the coast was clear. Surely, if they popped up that quickly, the dust storms would disappear just as swiftly and we'd be back on our way. As the flight continued and the sun grew lower, my hopes for a turnaround faded. Soon, we were taxiing back down the runway to the terminal in La Paz and we'd had not so much as a peep from the pilot since his initial announcement. The passengers around me dutifully filed off the plane without fuss or discussion. I was beginning to think that this must happen fairly regularly, as nobody except me seemed surprised, bemused or outraged. I shuffled along behind the rest of the passengers back into the terminal and I had no choice but to follow the crowd. I had no idea what the plan was now. Do we sit and wait for the flight to be cleared again? What happens to our luggage? How long might we be waiting? Will they try to add us onto another flight altogether? As everyone filed back inside and out of the wind, they seemed to be heading for the luggage carousel. Without a fuss, and as though it was the most normal thing in the world, everyone ahead of me simply collected their bags and either sat down or (more alarmingly for me, in my confused state) headed out of the terminal altogether. Why were people leaving? What the hell was going on? What were we supposed to do now, luggage in hand and still very much NOT IN FUCKING UYUNI?

I sat dejectedly in the baggage area for what seemed like an eternity, but was most probably only another 15 or 20 minutes, before finally an airport official of some sort arrived. He, like the pilot, spoke first in Spanish and then for my benefit in English (I was still giving off that *don't-try-to-speak-to-me-in-Spanish-I-can't-understand-you* vibe). He explained once again about the dust storm and that the flight would be rescheduled for tomorrow morning. Six am. Tomorrow. Fucking. Morning. *Fantastic.* FUCK YOU BOLIVIA! I rose slowly from my seat, my will to be outraged waning, and headed out of the terminal to find yet another taxi and yet another hostel for the night.

I used the wi-fi in the airport lounge (one of the few places in Bolivia that actually believed in the power of wi-fi, it seemed) and booked a cheap but apparently clean and safe hostel as close to the city centre as I could manage. I checked into my dark, cold and damp room with a view to two things; sleep and food. Not necessarily in that order. I checked the shower to find that it heralded gloriously luke-warm water and took my second shower for the day, only to find that within two minutes the water was stone cold freezing again. I almost laughed as I stepped out, freezing, and used the (you guessed it) threadbare towel to dry myself off and get dressed again. The heater didn't appear to work either, and so I put on every warm item of clothing that I could wear without looking like a bag lady and headed downstairs in search of food. Being in the city centre this time around (rather than in the sticks, as was the case in Santa Cruz) meant that my options were vastly improved. There were chain-store takeaways, little local restaurants and cafes to choose from. I didn't have the energy to appreciate a local restaurant (they all seemed to serve Italian anyway) and so I chose one of the chain-store chicken joints which displayed posters of McDonald's-esque meal deals with drinks and fries. I ordered who-knows-what and sat to wait for my food. What came out looked nothing remotely like anything in the back-lit light box photos behind the counter, but I ate it and sipped at my drink until I was bored enough to head back outside and into the streets for a wander.

I walked for a few blocks, perusing the ubiquitous *farmacia*, which, like everywhere else I'd been in South America, appeared at least once on every block, if not twice. I browsed souvenir shops with their half-hearted merchandise of Cholita dolls and keyrings, bangles and leather bracelets. By now I had such distaste for Bolivia (again, perhaps unfairly) that I decided to forego my usual new-country purchase of a hideous magnet for the fridge at home. Bolivia's magnets could fuck off. Once I'd ventured as far as I dared to go, I headed back for my dingy, cold hostel. Still fully dressed, I pulled out my book and spent the rest of the night reading by the barely luminous globe of my lamp before finally falling asleep.

The next morning, up bright and early (albeit decidedly less refreshed than the morning before), I headed back to the airport to try for Uyuni again. This time, thankfully, the flight took off and landed without incident and before I knew it I was thrust out into the cold, barren wasteland of outer Uyuni. HUZZAH!

The few taxi drivers hanging around had a captive audience of no more than a dozen tourists who didn't already have lifts. Because the airport was a good 25-minute drive from the town centre, there was little choice but to pay the exorbitant fare and head into the little metropolis. My hotel was further out, on the other side of the city. However, I needed to sort out my salt flats tour before I checked in. I was hoping to be able to book a tour to start the next day, as I was due to head out of Uyuni in four days. I asked the driver to just drop me in the middle of town, and I found myself luckily among a street of travel agents – Bolivian Style. Men and women dotted the street, touting for business and hustling tourists as they arrived from the airport or alternatively, were dropped off after long bus rides. I saw four-wheel drive cars loaded with eager faces heading out of town after hastily loading gear and backpacks on top of the cabins. I was determined this time not to be ripped off by unscrupulous persons and I put my hardest *don't-fuck-with-me* face on as I entered my first storefront and perused their posters. A weather-worn woman with leathery skin and a somber expression approached me and asked if I was going to the salt flats. Yes, I replied, and I wanted a two- or three-day tour with a group. She gave me the price (written down, as I still had trouble understanding) and it seemed quite reasonable based on what I'd read. She then asked me where I was staying, and offered to have the driver pick me up from there in the morning – saving me a cab fare. Excellent! But I was not going to be so hasty as to accept the first offer that came my way, and so I told her that I would shop around and come back to her if I didn't find something better. I didn't. Turns out no one else would offer to pick me up from my hotel for free, and so I went back to her, deposit in hand and paid her. Reassuringly, she wrote me a receipt and then told me to meet the driver outside at 10:00 am the next morning where I'd be picked up. Phew, sorted!

There seemed to be very little in the way of accommodation in Uyuni, and what little there was seemed to be booked out. I couldn't find a decent-looking hostel in town when I'd again used the airport wi-fi to search that morning before my flight. I was soon very glad that I hadn't left it to chance, as I could have been stuck without a room for the night if I'd chosen to just play it by ear as usual. Instead, I'd booked into an extremely overpriced hotel which sat outside town and was made almost entirely of salt from the surrounding landscape. The result was a *Star Wars*-ish feel of out-of-this-world architecture. Beds, benches, tables, walls; all were made of salt. It was quite beautiful actually, although it meant that everything was freezing cold to the touch, including the beds. The rooms were fitted out with heaters, which were of the not-quite-adequate variety, but were better than nothing.

As there was nothing to do outside the hotel grounds (except freeze), I contented myself with a hot shower (hallelujah!), then proceeded to spend the next several hours trying to connect to the abysmal wi-fi and wandering the building inspecting the many little alcoves and sitting areas in the hope of a stronger signal. Finally, after I'd taken a nap to pass yet more time, dinner was served at the in-house restaurant. For neither the first nor the last time on this trip, I began to wonder about the merits of travelling alone. I was given one of the best tables in the house, overlooking the sparse and rolling landscape of the Uyuni wilderness. When the waiter removed the spare cutlery, side plate and wine glass from my table I felt pangs of regret that I didn't have someone here to share the experience with. My outward veneer of confidence and solo-traveller-bravado began to wane and I felt a knot rise in my throat. I swallowed hard and willed myself not to cry there in that restaurant, well-lit and packed with other loved-up tourists. I'd dreamed of being such an intrepid adventurer. I'd spent nights marvelling at blogs and guidebooks and off-the-beaten-track websites about wild and windswept retreats, and hoping that one day I'd see myself there; dusty and grimy, backpack carelessly strung over one shoulder. There I was, in one of the most foreign and jarring places in the world. In a place that I was proud to stamp into my passport due to its sheer *otherness* and unpredictability. Here I was, and all I could think about was going home; curling into my own bug-free bed next to my husband and sleeping a long, deep sleep. Sleeping long enough to forget about this silly idea that I'd had; to travel to the other side of the world, to take off alone when plans failed. To sleep long enough to wake up and have forgotten all about it. To wake up and start dreaming all over again; dreaming up a better plan – a plan that would mean I wasn't alone.

* * * *

The next morning there was no time for self-pity. I had to savour one last hot shower, pack my things and wait for my driver. At 10:00 am I was to be picked up from the front of the hotel in what would be my transport for the next three days, and with my new travelling part-ners. I was excited and nervous all at once. Excited to be part of a small group, with whom I'd be seeing the sights and sharing the experiences of the salt flats with, and yet nervous as to whether we'd get along. I was desperate for some meaningful interaction with people, rather than just a passing comment or misinterpreted dinner order. I wanted to make friends.

Ten o'clock came and went. Still no sign of the driver. I sat awkwardly atop a boulder outside the hotel in the freezing weather and the blinding sunlight which reflected from every salt-encrusted surface. I dared not go back inside to wait in the (relative) warmth, lest the driver come past and assume I'd decided against coming. With no phone signal and little wi-fi, I'd sent off a Facebook message to Joel letting him know I'd most likely be incommunicado for the next four days. If my lift didn't show up, I'd be forced to spend another night in the hotel I could scarcely afford or head back into town to confront the travel agent who'd sold me my ticket. Most likely to little avail, as Bolivians were notorious for not issuing refunds (and I wasn't keen to repeat my crazy-woman sketch from the Santa Cruz depot any time soon). I didn't have time to argue for a booking on another trip, as I'd be on a bus out of Uyuni before I could complete it.

All I could do was sit and wait in the cold and resort to pacing around my boulder to get my blood pumping. Minute after excruciating minute I waited until finally, a cloud of dust rounding the corner suggested the approach of a vehicle. Soon (though not soon enough) a four-wheel drive bowled up to the hotel entrance in a puff of dust and salt, and out jumped the driver. I tried to hide the desperation and relief that I felt as he asked for my name and seemed satisfied that I was indeed the right Maggie. He took my pack and hoisted it onto the top of the vehicle with the rest of the luggage and gestured for me to get inside. There were already five other people squeezed into the vehicle, four of whom were in the back seat. The driver didn't seem to notice an issue, and hopped into his seat ready to take off. I studied my new companions and awkward greetings were exchanged before room was hastily made in the front seat next to a strawberry-blonde haired girl who seemed to be in her mid-20s. I felt self-conscious about the room my ass took up on the seat and noted quickly, as I do without fail, that each and every other passenger was slimmer and fitter looking than me. The only bonus of the freezing conditions out there was that my makeup stayed put and afforded me a small boost in confidence as it hid the imperfections in my skin and made me look a little less unwashed-hillbilly and a little more backpacker-chic.

As I donned the beanie and gloves I had picked up in town the day before, the other guests and I swapped the regular details over the noise of the engine. Name, where we were from, how long we'd be away, where we were going next. Beau and her boyfriend Roy were straight from the Dutch central casting catalogue under headings 'Gorgeous, vivacious blonde journalist' and 'Ex-military, tall-dark-and-handsome adventurer type'. The other three guests were a British trio on extended leave from home. Stephan, his girlfriend Rebecca and his sister Marie-Claire (strawberry-blonde) were two months in to a six-month trip around South America. I was instantly jealous and felt more than a little sixth-wheel. As talk is hard over the rumbling of the Jeep and rattling of the wheels over the rough terrain, we all leant back silently, exchanging the occasional grin or grimace as we hurtled along.

First stop for that day was around lunch time, as we reached an apparently pre-designated spot, which was for all intents and purposes totally barren of identifiable features. Fernando, our driver, bounded from the car and set about pulling boxes and equipment from the back. He gestured to the surrounding flats and for the first time I realised that this was, in fact, the spot at which many a famous photo was taken. For miles in every direction was the crusty, bare white earth on which many a photo-gag was enacted. As Fernando prepared lunch, we each pulled out our cameras and posed for funny pictures. Roy ran off in to the distance as Beau, in the foreground, pretended to hold his tiny frame atop her hand. I took photos for the others, and each of them kindly helped me pose for my own and offered themselves as props for some optical-illusions. Standard tourist photos taken (including one where I appeared to be stepping on and squishing a tiny Roy in the distance) we then sat down for lunch. We ate rice and vegetables and, to my surprise, alpaca! I was always keen to try new and interesting foods for the brag-factor and happily chomped away at the lamb-like steak. That's another foreign fare I could tick off my list.

After more driving and a quick stop at the 'Cactus Island' we arrived late in the afternoon at our accommodation for the night. Not much to look at, the concrete compound was sparsely decorated with a few tables and chairs in the common area and rooms with single beds piled high with blankets. Just our luck, as the compound had no heating and the electricity cut out after dark. After venturing outside to watch the magnificent sunset, we spent the rest of the evening huddled around small tables, sipping tea and getting to know each other better, before each heading wearily to bed. As I was alone, I got a room to myself, and quickly jumped under the covers after locking the door (in a bring-your-own-padlock arrangement).

The blankets were blissfully warm and I drifted off to sleep without too much trouble.

That night I experienced my first and only ever night-terror. I'd heard of these worse-than-a-simple-nightmare type of scenarios, as my little brother used to have them as a young kid. I opened my eyes to the pitch-dark room and saw nothing, but suddenly became aware of a large figure on top of me and holding me down. I felt a pillow over my face and was completely unable to move. As I tried to breathe, I felt my chest crushing under the weight of this invisible stranger on top of me and it took me many moments to compose myself and muster enough energy to scream with all of my might.

Instantly, I was properly awake. A limp but heavy pillow lying by my side, the room still dark and yet not so dark that I couldn't see that I was completely alone in the room; padlock still intact, and room still secure. I'd obviously pulled the pillow over myself for warmth, and my brain had concocted a horrible explanation for the weight on my torso. I waited to hear stirrings and mutters from outside, wondering whether I'd woken anyone up. As it seemed, my scream must also have been a part of my dream, as I heard not a whisper from outside the room. Grateful that I hadn't embarrassed myself publicly, I panted and eventually brought my breath back down to a normal rate. Once again, I drifted off to sleep.

The next morning the group and I breakfasted in the common room before bundling up once again into the Jeep for our first full day of adventures. We visited the famous coloured lakes of Bolivia, one green, one blue, one red. We watched pink flamingoes in their hundreds flock and bathe and pick at the algae which gave them their rosy colour. It was truly something out of a postcard, although it stunk to high heavens! Much to my relief, I got along well with all of my companions. Most especially with Beau and Roy, who proved to be generous, thoughtful and friendly beyond measure. Each of them jumped in with an offer to take a photo, or better yet, pose with me when the opportunity for a good shot arose, and I repaid them by dutifully ensuring they got countless couple-shots at the various natural attractions. I couldn't thank them enough for the way they accommodated me, and never once let me feel left-out or burdensome.

We saw some incredible scenery that day, as we toured the coloured lakes of Bolivia. Laguna Verde was first – the green lake. A magnificent expanse of the deepest, most surreal greens and blues imaginable. Flamingoes dotted the shoreline and each of us marvelled at the beauty of this remote place. A couple of hours further along, we came to Laguna Colorado, the red lake. Just as spectacular, this lake looks like something from Mars. It is so completely alien looking. Here, thousands upon thousands of flamingoes crowded around the shores, eating the algae that gave them their intense colouring. Now it was obvious; I was standing at the spot where so many *National Geographic* shots of the famous flamingoes had been taken. It was like I was standing inside a postcard. Just as incredible as the scenery was the stench! Holy moly, it's powerful. And all-pervading. The fierce winds ripped through our hair and tore at our clothes, ensuring that down on the shores there was no escaping the reek. As amazed as we all were at the incredible views, before long each of us was gagging a little and retreated to the top of the hill where the smell was less pervasive, and the wind less savage. What a sight!

What an experience! I was now, finally, starting to relax and enjoy the trip. These were the kinds of sights that I'd dreamed about seeing. I was cold, smelly, a million miles from anywhere – and loving it. It was a relief to have some new friends to share it with.

That night in our second 'hotel' (for really, it was just another, smaller, concrete compound) we all sat up telling travel stories. I'd brought a pack of Uno cards, the universal leveller and perfect for team-building activities. I patted myself silently on the back for that great act of forethought, as everyone was soon laughing and arguing, cheating and competing. Over cups of tea and the light of our smartphones (the generator was switched off after dark) we swapped war stories of travel mishaps, and made regular brave trips to the pitch-dark bathrooms. We laughed and chatted the night away until all of our phones finally died and we had no option left but to head to bed. This time, we were all packed into a dorm-style room with beds lined up against the wall and bags slung across the odd table or chair. It was a very school-camp type of atmosphere and one of the best nights of my trip. I slept contented that night, and night-terror free.

Our last day was spent seeing more of the sights as we drove for hours, passing through national parks and having to get our passports stamped and pay a fee to see much of what we'd already seen for free. At one of our stops we met a couple who pulled up on bicycles with over-laden panniers covered in stickers to mark what presumably were the many countries they'd visited. It turned out they were cycling through the whole of North and South America from top to bottom on their bicycles. It was the stuff of my dreams, and as they pulled away after answering our questions and directing us to their website, I admired their adventure greatly. What a trip! Like many others, I filed that adventure dream away in the mental cabinet with all of the rest; hoping that one day I'd sift through those folders and pull it out again, ready to take a chance on something like that.

Our trip drew to an end, and finally, we rolled back into Uyuni proper as the sunlight was starting to fade and the restaurants around town turned their lights on in hope of evening diners. Beau and Roy were off to catch an early bus out of town, and we said goodbye, swapping email addresses and promising to add each other to Facebook. I had a couple of hours to kill until my bus was due to depart, and so after a visit to an internet café, the three Brits and I found a pub and stopped for a drink and some food before it was time to say another goodbye. As the time came for me to find my bus, the three of them walked me to the bus stop and helped me find the right travel agent to collect my ticket from. Signage was terrible, and my Spanish was worse, so I was eternally grateful when Stephan enquired within and confirmed that my bus was outside and waiting for passengers to board. With more hugs, email address exchanges and goodbyes, I boarded my bus and found my seat. I waved goodbye to them as they walked back into town and out of view.

I wasn't lucky enough to score a window seat for this trip, and had to content myself with the aisle while my next-door-neighbour set up his bus-trip paraphernalia in his seat; squishy neck pillow, full sized pillow, 2-litre bottle of water, headphones and iPad. I whipped out my own squishy neck pillow and book and stashed the rest of my belongings under the seat in front. This was to be an 11-hour ride north through Bolivia, back the way I'd flown a few days earlier, to La Paz. Finally, I was going to have that long bus ride in Bolivia that I'd evaded so far (albeit, this one with food and a toilet, although no reclining seats). Promisingly, the bus took off on time and before long we were offered refreshments by a young boy who sat up near the driver and whose sole purpose seemed to be to serve food and drink and then simply keep the driver company. It worked for me. I finished my snack (packet of nondescript biscuits and a cup of tea) and settled in to read my book before deciding to save my phone battery and turn my torch-light off.

Bolivian roads are an adventure in themselves. They really have to be experienced to be understood. Then again, understood is probably not the word for it. It was as though the Bolivian government had undertaken a strange scientific experiment (for the advancement of the human race, of course) in constructing a road entirely out of potholes. It was more hole than road. It was the anti-road. Like black matter. Or something like that. Anyway, the result was that passengers needed to strap themselves tightly down with their seatbelts to avoid being thrown bodily into the aisles at regular intervals. You could almost set your watch by the timed bounces, bumps and slams of the bus wheels into hole after hole. Some of them almost big enough to swallow a bus. One. Two. Three. Four. SMASH. One. Two. Three. Four. SLAM.

By some miracle, I managed to fall asleep, but not for long. I'd shifted and squished and executed acts worthy of circus performers until, one leg over the other and knees pinned against the chair in front of me, I'd dozed off. After what seemed like only moments into this new position (it hadn't been long enough for my legs to go dead, and that's the only measure of time I had, besides the one, two, three BUMP clock), I was woken abruptly by a large and heavy object hitting me SMACK on the top of the head. Extricating myself within a millisecond from my repose, I panned the bus, bug-eyed, looking for the culprit. A 2-litre water bottle rattled down the aisle. No one else had stirred during this ordeal, least of all my neighbour, whose water bottle had been not-so-securely stored in the overhead racks, it seemed.

No feat of flexibility or super-human double-jointedness would have seen me fall back to sleep on that long night, and there was nothing for it but to turn my phone back on and read my book by its light until we arrived. After an eleven-hour journey, we pulled into the bus terminal-cum-carpark at La Paz and I wearily bundled myself and my backpack off the bus. The other passengers seemed to have an idea where they were headed and filed off unceremoniously into the distance or were greeted by family and friends. I on the other hand, ever the baffled tourist, was accosted by a myriad of taxi drivers and touts. I didn't much care by this stage. I simply wanted a shower, a change of clothes and a bed. I pulled one driver from the throng, handed him the name of a hostel I'd read about and sat, bleary-eyed in the back seat as we sped through the streets of the city.

I spent the final night in that country curled up in my hostel bed, too tired to do much of anything. I slept long and deep until my alarm woke me at stupid o'clock the next morning and I made my way to a Bolivian airport for the last time to board a plane out of this place once and for all.

And with the flourish of a stamp and a walk through the terminal to my plane, it was *GOODBYE BOLIVIA!*

10

Feet Give Out
(Great Ocean Walk, Australia)

As you'll remember, I was curled up at the carpark on the Great Ocean Walk, awaiting my Knights in Shining Armour Four to collect me and deposit me at Aire River. I still hadn't encountered any serial killers. Phew! I had spread out my ground tarp and made myself comfortable, waiting for the guys to return. A couple of cars pulled into the car park and people headed down the cliff towards the beach for what I assumed was fishing and swimming. I didn't give any of them much more than a glance. I wasn't ready to answer questions about what I was doing up there all alone, I wasn't ready for the company of day-trippers. My appearance and my inevitable haven't-showered-in-three-days stench was not the best recipe for pleasant interactions and I didn't want to encourage anyone by meeting their gaze with my usual cheery smile for strangers. My pack rested next to me and afforded me some measure of explanation. It was quite obvious that I was a hiker, and with a large pack and the state of my appearance it was (I hoped) equally as obvious that I was on more than a day-hike. I relied on people's general insular manner which meant that in groups or pairs they were less likely to interact with someone on their own who was clearly there for a purpose far removed from theirs. It all worked in my favour and I wasn't approached by anybody. I got a simple 'G'day' from one man who appeared to be a park ranger, checking up on something down by the beach. He jumped back into his truck and was off in a flash after he'd completed whatever he'd been there to do. I like to think that if I'd clearly needed help, any of those people would have lent a hand without hesitation. But at that moment, I was content to sit alone and wait, and gather my thoughts.

After my intrepid (ha!) solo travels in South America, I'd considered myself to be a fairly capable traveller – at least able to extricate myself from a sticky situation with minimal fuss and agitation (ok, so perhaps with maximum fuss and a few handy swear words). This walk was really getting the better of me. I tried hard to remind myself that this must happen to a lot of hikers. I'd read many an account of giant blisters and sprained ankles and knew that in reality, even experienced long-distance hikers had their share of maladies. Better to admit defeat while I was in a position to find help, than to continue on and perhaps realise my mistake too late – while alone and without a car for miles.

I had barely been waiting an hour before a station wagon rolled up beside me and The Four Blokes piled out.

"Wow, I can't believe how fast you got here!" I grinned to the first of them.

"You been ok sitting up here?" he asked.

"Yeah. I barely got out my e-reader and set up my tarp and you're here already!"

They offered me the shotgun seat, and I felt a little guilty as three of them squeezed into the back. It would have been more awkward with me squeezed in among two of them, I decided, and happily took the seat up front. We chatted about hiking, about how Bec and I met and they exclaimed their shock at how quick Bec was.

"She kept up pace with us for a while there. She's pretty fast!" one of the guys in the back explained.

"So she's doing ok then? You don't think she'll have any trouble making it to Aire River alone?" I was still worried about the moral ambiguities around leaving her to hike on alone while I hitched a ride with a bunch of strangers in the middle of nowhere to a spot where I'd never been, and with no phone signal to speak of. I wasn't sure who was in more danger, Bec or me. I also wasn't sure if either of us should feel as though we'd not fulfilled our unspoken friendship traveller duties of never leaving another man behind. There's an unspoken girls' rule that you don't leave a girl on her own when you go out at night, too. Was this the same? Did we really have a choice? We were both grown-ups, and we'd each made our own decision. Bec wouldn't have hiked on if she was uncomfortable with the idea. I wouldn't have stayed behind if I thought I could make it to civilisation and a phone on foot. Our consciences were both clear, I decided. At least until tonight. Let's see what happened.

The Four Blokes were friendly and encouraging, telling me (like Suzanne had) that it happens to everybody. It turns out that they'd been hiking the GOW since they were teens together, and they came back for a long weekend whenever each of them could get away from work, wives, and kids. They were seriously experienced hikers, and told me how tough the rest of that day would have been if I'd tried to continue. By the end of the half-hour car ride, I was definitely reassured that I'd made the right decision and I felt a little less ridiculous. Although, I'm pretty sure they were just trying to make me feel better, and had probably never been reduced to a situation similar to mine. Nonetheless, I felt relieved and a little validated. Self-deprecation has always been a character trait of mine, and I found that rather than trying to hide my struggles and disappointment with myself, it felt better to simply admit my weaknesses and let anyone who'd listen know that I simply was not prepared for how difficult this walk would be.

After many an unsealed, jumpy dirt road we made it to the Aire River turnoff. They drove me right up to the ancient, wooden, rickety and (surely not) load-bearing bridge; and despite my protestations and assurances that I could walk across it myself, they insisted on driving across it and dropping me as close as they could to the campsite. Really, the driver just saw that insane excuse for a bridge as a bit of an adrenaline rush and wanted to see if we'd make it across without plummeting into the river.

Each of us held our breath and were soon (not soon enough) over it. They lifted my pack out of the boot and bid me adieu and best wishes, and then rattled back over the bridge in a cloud of dust. I took a photo of the back of the car as they disappeared past the bridge. I wanted to remember that ride. Even if I couldn't remember their names.

I approached the campsite alone and was eager to set up my gear in preparation for Bec's arrival. I wanted to make things as easy as possible for when she finally walked into camp. Despite her fitness and the ease with which she was making miles, I knew that it was a huge day for her and that she'd be exhausted when she finally arrived. As I slowly made my way up the wooden stair-like structure to the raised hike-in campground (Parks Victoria have a sadistic sense of humour, I'm sure), I was wondering what kind of people I might find in camp that night. Suzanne and Graham were taking a day out at a caravan park in a nice cabin and with a few bottles of red, I'm sure. They'd asked me to come and stay there too, if I needed a break. As tempting as it was, logistically I couldn't organise it. It appeared we wouldn't see them again on this hike, and we'd bid each other a warm goodbye that morning as I'd left camp behind Bec. I'd miss them, and I was so glad to have met them.

As I came upon the campsites at Aire River there appeared to already be a large group of people on site. I could see a couple of men sitting on one of the large benches and could make out mutterings of others setting up their camps surrounding the entrance. As I drew closer, still hobbling, one of the men on the bench lifted his head in surprise.

"You're not one of ours!" he said, with a large grin. He was wearing a weather-worn Akubra, a tank top and a pair of speedo y-fronts. And nothing else. He sat lazily, eating a bowl of something, and sat upright as I came closer.

"Ah, no. Not one of yours." I grinned back.

"Where have you come from then?" he ventured. Ah, I thought, complicated question. How much detail is one required to go into in such a situation? I could have told him I'd come from Blanket Bay, but with my complete inability to lie or to be seen to be taking credit for something I hadn't actually achieved (for some weird misplaced fear of being caught out and humiliated?), I couldn't bring myself to do it. Instead, I hazarded a short version of the story.

"I started at Blanket Bay this morning. But I didn't make it the whole way on foot. I just got a lift from near Cape Otway." Close enough to the full story, I figured. The whole story might just send him to sleep.

"Oh, I see. Blisters?"

Bingo! Perhaps there's no need for a full explanation to other hikers. They get it. I nodded in assent, and then gave a shrug of resignation and defeat. "I guess I'd better go set up camp, so when my friend gets in she can take a break," I added, and then made my way through the site to find a nice spot for the night.

This was a beautiful campsite. Close enough to the drive-in site, in case of emergency, which gave me hope of being able to maybe find a solution for tomorrow. I hardly thought my feet were going to heal overnight and I still needed a plan for the rest of the trip. The individual sites were all nestled among the trees and long grass. It was warmer here than it had been the previous few nights, which meant that tonight's sleep might be a little easier.

And to boot, some of the sites had padded ground mats and sand beneath; a much more comfortable night, by the look of things!

I busied myself by setting up my tent, leaving plenty of room for Bec's tent, and then I set about unpacking the rest of my gear and arranging it in the appropriate places; ready for tea making, dinner preparations, and the like. Within ten minutes of having things set up, my Akubra-clad friend was sitting at the bench near that campsite I'd claimed, and started chatting as if we were old buddies.

"So, do you think you can hike without a pack? We have two options for tomorrow. First, I can carry your pack and you can walk. Or second, I can carry you." He looked at me expectantly. This is the way he opened the conversation. We'd known each other less than an hour and he was offering to carry my pack, and/or ME. I stifled a laugh, lest I offended him. I instantly liked him and couldn't believe that within moments of walking into camp that day, I'd found someone who was already trying to help me overcome my predicament. The kindness of strangers, hey?

"Ah, well, I'm not sure I'll make it even without my pack. My feet are shot. And you definitely can't carry all 80kg of me!" He was only a slim guy, albeit tall and clearly fit. "I really need to get a lift to Johanna Beach tomorrow, I think. So I'm hoping I can figure something out."

"Don't you worry," he waved a nonchalant hand at me. "We'll sort it out. I'm off to get some wine for everyone. I'll be back soon and we'll chat," and with that he was off. I only discovered later, after talking to several of the other hikers that he'd actually run back to his car (that's right RUN – to the next campsite some 14 ks away) and then driven it back, only to then drive it to Johanna Beach that night and run back AGAIN to Aire River. He was a machine! No wonder he was only wearing y-fronts, a tank top and carrying no gear: he was just running from his car and back each day! Mental! I was impressed if not a bit envious.

Just as Bec rolled into camp (exhausted), Will (for that was his name) appeared at our site, set down a bottle of wine and a packet of biscuits, winked and was off to sort out his plans to drive his car back to Johanna Beach and head back again. Bec was confused, but instantly won over by the wine and snacks from this effusive stranger. I explained to her about Will while we set up her gear and then headed down to the picnic area for some dinner.

As we walked down, we caught Will just as he was about to head off. We chatted about my options for the next day and as we were talking, a little woman with dark hair and a bucket hat walked past. She stopped and turned as she overheard what we were discussing, and without so much as thinking she asked, "Are you trying to get to Johanna Beach tomorrow?" Yes, I nodded. "Well we're heading there tomorrow; we've got our caravan. You can come with us!" My eyes lit up and I beamed with relief and enthusiasm. I looked to her and then Will and then back to her, hardly able to believe my luck. "Just pop on down and see us later, and we'll organise a plan. We're in the A-van down there." She gestured back down the hill towards the drive-in sites. I gushed my thanks and promised to head down after she'd had dinner in half an hour or so. With that, Will gave me a smile and a look that said, "There, see? Sorted!" and was off into the night in his Speedos.

That wine was just about the best thing Bec and I had ever tasted, and with the bottle between us, we were quite cheery and red-cheeked. We had a great time, and attracted other hikers and caravanners as they walked through the picnic area to and from the bathrooms. It felt like being at a school camp once again, where everyone knows each other. We all talked as if we'd been acquaintances for years. As I've said before, hikers have everything in common and plenty to talk about. It was just a fabulous night and we were feeling great – plus, the wine didn't hurt.

With my wine-buzz, I decided that the large group of hikers who were sitting at the bench a few yards away from ours would be a wealth of knowledge about the Great Ocean Walk. They were the group Will was with, and although each of them was between the ages of 45 and 65, all appeared to be seasoned walkers. With bravado, I picked up my GOW map, walked over to them and laid it down on the grass at their feet.

"I need your help," I said, as I laid out the map. Instantly a few of them hunched over it with me as I explained my predicament.

"I've got a lift to Johanna Beach sorted tomorrow, but I need to know what my options are after that. I've got no phone signal, and so can't call anyone to organise anything. How does a girl get around out here without a phone? Do I need to try and catch another lift from Johanna Beach? What do you think I should do?"

Well, as far as information went, I'd hit the jackpot. Tony and his partner Lisa had hiked the GOW many times. They were on a weekend hike with the rest of their party, and all of them were training for an Oxfam event. The idea is to walk 100 ks in 28 hours – non-stop – to raise money. Seasoned walkers was an understatement – these were seriously fit folk. I was a little in awe of them.

"Well, you can just catch a ride with Abby. No need to worry about the phone. He's picking us up from Johanna Beach at 1:00 pm tomorrow and we're heading home. You can talk to him then and he'll sort you out!" Tony explained. Abby, it turned out, was the one and only GOW shuttle operator, and Lisa assured me that he'd have no trouble picking me up from Johanna Beach.

"He'll always fit you in, don't worry!" she offered, when I looked concerned. Not having a mobile phone was really testing my resolve. I couldn't simply email, search and credit-card my way out of the situation and it was making me nervous. But so far, the kindness and openness of other hikers (and caravanners) had proven infallible, and I was assured by the group that I had nothing to worry about. I put my reservations aside and decided to trust their advice and just go with the flow. It would all be ok.

With Bec back at camp, getting ready for bed, I got changed into some new clothes and shortly headed down to find the lady who'd offered me a lift. Luckily, they were the only A-van in the campsite, and I could see them from across the field, lights on and sitting down at their little dining table inside the van. I nervously rounded the van and made a little knock on the door, trying not to rattle it too much.

"Come on in!" she called. Geraldine introduced herself and her husband, Phil as I opened up the door and climbed the two stairs into the tiny, candlelit room. "Shut the door behind you. There's lots of mozzies out tonight."

I did as I was told and suddenly was sharing a 1.5-metre square space, almost leaning up against the bed as Geraldine and Phil sat opposite at the table.

"This is Maggie, Phil," Geraldine offered as I shook Phil's hand warmly. He smiled and I felt instantly at ease. These were warm, generous and gracious folk. Geraldine had already explained to Phil that I'd be travelling with them tomorrow, and all seemed to be arranged without a fuss. She told me to come and meet them at around 11:00 am the next day, after they'd gone for 'a bit of a walk' after breakfast, and we'd head off from there. I'm a stickler for detail, and not being left behind was quite important and vital to my survival, so I checked and double checked the details and gave them backup options for where to find me, should I miss them or should they finish early. I promised to be waiting in the picnic area no later than 10:00 am, in case they wanted to leave earlier. Phil smiled a sympathetic smile.

"Don't worry," he said, sensing my anxiety. "We won't leave without you."

Plans laid and my mind at ease, I bid them good-night and headed back to my tent. Bec was sitting up in bed, reading. She was still in a good mood from the wine and fine conversation we'd had. I daresay the warmth of the air and the comfort underfoot also had something to do with it as well. It had truly been a wonderful night, and in my mind, was what camping was all about. She gave me a grin, and we sat up, tent doors facing each other, chatting and laughing. I explained to her the plan, and she was content to walk on the next day and meet me at Johanna Beach. It shouldn't be too long of a day for her, and we expected she'd arrive by around midday.

* * * *

Next morning, I woke to the sound of a herd of footsteps passing our site. It was still dark. There had been a group of school students on a hike staying nearby in one of the group sites last night, and it looked as though they were off to an early start. Lying back and trying to pretend I might still get some more sleep in, the birds soon started chirping and the usual morning noises of the bush joined in. Around that time, my bladder decided it was time to rise as well, and there was nothing for it but to get up and welcome the day.

I had hoped that by some miracle my feet might have healed overnight; however it was not to be, and I painfully hobbled down the tree-trunks-cum-stairs to the bathrooms. When I arrived back, Bec was up and going about her morning rituals of gear-packing and not eating breakfast. This didn't dissuade me, and I went about making porridge as usual. I was in no hurry today. Despite sore and battered feet, I was in good spirits, as I knew that I needn't worry about hiking that day. I felt a guilty pleasure in knowing that I simply had to catch my ride, set up camp and laze about for the rest of the afternoon at Johanna Beach. Bec was pumped too, I could tell, and was eager to get going. Today for her meant that she could finally go at her own pace and test herself, without me holding her back. She packed quickly and as we heard Will's group about to set off, she hurried to catch up with them. Once she'd gone, I lazily packed down my tent and enjoyed the warmth of the sunshine creeping over the trees and into the campsite. The weather was fine and I was happy, relieved to be taking a rest day and finally (I hoped) enjoying my surroundings without the constant burning, searing pain of blisters and torn muscles to distract me.

By the time I'd packed, I was alone in the campsite. I headed down to the group picnic area where we'd had dinner the night before and sat to read my book until Geraldine and Phil were ready to take off. I still had the tiniest amount of nervousness about the arrangement, although in my heart I knew they wouldn't leave without me. I wasn't really comfortable yet with relying entirely on someone else for my welfare, and without a phone as backup, at that! At around 10:00 am, as the weather had turned a little grey, I decided to take a stroll over to where the A-van was parked, just to check that it was still there. I could see Phil busying himself packing things down, and he greeted me warmly as I approached.

"Already been out for your walk this morning?" I asked.

"Yes, a little one," he said, "although it was a bit too cold this morning. So we're going to go for a quick one once we've packed up here and we'll be ready to leave at about 10:30 am or 11:00 am. We'll come back and get you then, before we leave."

I sighed inaudibly with relief, and organised to wait at the shelter just outside of the carpark for them – that way there was no way they could make a getaway without me spotting them. It's not that I have trust issues. Actually, I tend to give people (pretty naively) the benefit of the doubt. But I do have this ever persistent fear that people will forget about me. Since I was a kid, I've always hesitated before saying hello to someone in the street, lest they've forgotten who I am completely. I never expect people to remember me and even at work when meeting clients for the fourth or fifth time, I'll introduce myself again just in case. I must remember to talk to my future therapist about this. Reminder to self: find therapist.

Back at the bench under the shelter I read my ebook while waiting for Geraldine and Phil. Soon enough, the van rolled around the corner and I stuffed my reader and other knick-knacks into my bag, ready to jump in. As Phil pulled the four-wheel drive up, he jumped out and scooted off behind the car to adjust something. Geraldine got out and made space for me in the back seat.

"I hope I'm not being any trouble," I offered. "I can't tell you how grateful I am for the lift!"

"Not at all! Don't be silly! We were just lucky that we were already planning on heading there ourselves. It's worked out great!" She put me at ease.

Finally, we were ready to head off and all bundled back into the car. Phil fumbled with the built-in GPS and I could tell that the car had been a recent purchase, along with the A-van. Soon enough, after a few turns and reverses to find the right exit (we were too heavy to go out over the wooden bridge, and I once again, sighed inaudibly in relief), we were out of sight of Aire River and on the road.

Ah, the feeling of flying past the scenery at driving speed when for days, I'd looked at every tiny rise and hill as just another excruciating obstacle to overcome. It was indescribable. I'd read many books about long walks, and the authors more often than not, would enthusiastically preach quite the opposite. Seeing the world at a snail's pace was meant to give you more time to appreciate everything you were passing, and hopping back in the car again afterwards would seem foreign, a waste, a blight of modernity on the wondrous natural world. Bah humbug! I was loving every moment of seeing the Victorian countryside at warp speed. Although to be fair, this was only about 20 ks per hour for the first few kilometres, as the unsealed roads wreaked havoc on the van behind us and it jostled noisily about. Geraldine, Phil and I chatted over the creaks, bangs and groans. They told me of their plans to travel around Australia; first stop after Victoria was Longreach in Queensland to visit their daughter, and then on to the Northern Territory. I was quite jealous actually, and imagined what it must be like to retire, and have all the time in the world (or what earthly time you have left) to wander around with your other half and enjoy the days with nothing much to do and nowhere in particular to be. No deadlines, no bosses, no other mundane responsibilities. Just time to enjoy yourself, and the vast expanse of *otherness* to explore.

Eventually, I was snapped out of my reverie as Geraldine announced that we were arriving at Johanna Beach. I'd assumed that, like Aire River, the campsite and carpark would be clearly designated and unmistakable. I was sorely disappointed as we rounded the bend, and a sprawling maze of trails, green fields and patches of sand lay before us. There were easily hundreds of metres of space which could be considered parking space, and I couldn't see any hike-in campsite signage at all. There were one or two other cars around, but I couldn't see any other hikers – or any other people at all, for that matter.

Phil parked up the van and offered to go on a hunt for signs and campgrounds, while I stressed about where on earth I would find Lisa and Tony, and my next lifeline: Abby. After a fruitless hunt up a set of steep stairs, Phil struck one track from the list of possibilities and dutifully filed off in search of another. I stayed behind, thankful to be given a reprieve from this searching on foot, as my feet wouldn't have handled much of it. Before long, I could see a shock of dark hair bobbing up from the beach and over the stairs. Within moments, Will appeared, clad as always, in his Speedos and tank top and not much else.

"Oh my God!" I exclaimed. "I can't believe you're here already! Did you run the whole way?"

"No, darling. But most of the way. The others aren't far behind!" He wiped sweat from his brow and took a long gulp from his water. I used this time to mine him for information about where on earth I'd meet the others, where Abby was likely to pull up and where the hike-in campgrounds were.

"Oh we just camped right there last time, darls. Nobody will bother you!" He pointed out a smooth patch of grass beside a day shelter and bench, and beside which was planted a sign that clearly stated, 'NO CAMPING'.

I looked at him forlornly. I'm a straighty-one-eighty from way back, and rule-breaking is NOT a pastime of mine. (Bribing border guards in desperate situations doesn't count!) I gave him a noncommittal response and secretly decided that there was no way on earth I was setting up camp next to that sign. Minutes later, more heads popped up over the top of the stairs, and eventually Tony and Lisa arrived. Phil was back from yet another fruitless hunt for the campsites, and we followed the others over to where they awaited pickup. In order to not miss Abby, and hence my lifeline for the next day, I had to stay nearby.

I assured Geraldine and Phil that I'd find out where to camp once Abby arrived (he'd be sure to know) and a motherly look came over Geraldine's face.

"How will we know that you're ok?" She grabbed a pen and insisted that I wrote my phone number on her hand, so that she could message me in a few days to make sure I made it back to civilisation and, presumably, a phone signal. I bid them both a warm goodbye and thanked them again for their generosity. They weren't staying, and said they'd simply wanted to get a look at Johanna Beach. But I really suspect they'd made the trip especially to drop me off. After hugs and final farewells, they were back in their car and on the road again. I never did hear from Geraldine, but I hope they're still trekking around the Australian outback in their A-van, and enjoying the far-flung places they'd hoped to visit.

11

Fookin' Falkirk!
(Scotland)

It was mid-January 2012. My friend Sarah and I had spent a spectacular three weeks travelling through Europe on a Contiki tour, visiting France, Germany, the Netherlands, Austria and Italy (to name but a few). Now we were headed back to London for the final ten days before I was due to return home. Sarah would be staying for another few weeks with an old friend outside of London, and I would be boarding a plane home by myself. This was to be the first time I'd ever flown long-haul alone (although of course, it was not to be my last).

We'd decided to book a car for five days which would allow us to see as much of the UK as we wanted to, without the tiresome restrictions of bus and train time-tables. After making our way through customs (Sarah had a British passport and so always made it through faster than I did), we found our way to the rental car depot to pick up our chariot. We'd booked a small two-door car, as really that was all the two of us needed, and we were at the tail-end of our trip with funds running short. The clerk at the depot had other ideas though, and offered us an upgrade at a 'very reasonable price' and frankly, her friendly demeanour and my complete and utter inability to say no got the better of me. Within minutes we'd agreed to upgrade to a Vauxhall something-or-other with built-in GPS and many other whizz-bang accessories we probably didn't need or wouldn't be able to figure out. Finally, before letting us go, she asked about our insurance options and whether we wanted to upgrade to 'zero liability'.

"No, no, I'm sure we'll be fine!" I'd chirped. (Look at that, I'd found my backbone!)

"Oh, but you don't understand," she explained. "Here we go …. you see, even if you're parked at a shopping centre and somebody opens their car door into yours; you're liable. The excess is 800 pounds."

Yikes, I thought! I do NOT have £800 to spare, should some numpty run a shopping trolley into our hire car. I discussed with Sarah, who agreed that it was probably the smartest thing to do. We split the cost of the extra insurance and soon had our keys in hand.

I still find it astonishing that you can be given the keys to a rental car in a foreign country and shown the parking lot without so much as instructions on how to find your car, let alone how to drive it, or even the most cursory enquiry as to whether or not you know which side of the road to drive on and how to read the road signs. Hand over a credit card and they'll let you figure it out yourself, it seems. After a bit of faffing around with switches and eventually discovering that the windscreen wiper knob was not, in fact, the headlights switch, we eventually had the engine turned on and the lights shining brightly into the bumpers of the row of cars adjacent to ours. I gingerly shifted the automatic gearstick into 'D' for drive (well at least, I hoped that's what 'D' meant in English cars) and pulled slowly from the car space. Driving out of the car lot and, terrifyingly, on to the open road, we headed north to find our hotel.

As Sarah was under 25 at the time, she wasn't even allowed in the driver's seat and so, the entirety of the driving was to be left to me. This didn't bother me at all; however, it did put an added amount of pressure on me. I really didn't want to be responsible for informing Sarah's parents of her untimely death at the hands of me and my nervous driving. Like a granny, I took the corners and the back roads slowly and steadily until we made it to our first stop: Manchester. It was getting pretty late by this stage and so after checking in we decided to hit the hay for the night and rise early the next day, with any luck refreshed and bright-eyed.

Early next morning, we did just that. Being back in England, where they considered in-room tea and coffee facilities to be a standard, we blissfully sipped at steaming cups of tea while peering out into the dreary English sub-urban weather outside. After the three weeks we'd spent trying to learn a dozen different languages, we'd decided that we'd spend the day lazily wandering the large shopping centre in town, stocking up on supplies and taking full advantage of the fact that everything was once again labelled in English.

We'd soon exhausted the pharmacies and browsed the aisles of Selfridges long enough, and with still many hours in the day to kill, we decided to catch a movie. The cinema complex on the top level of the centre was impressive and I revelled in a large diet coke and popcorn as we sat down in the giant theatre to watch *The Girl with the Dragon Tattoo*. I'd been given the book years earlier by Sarah's older sister, my friend Mandy. She'd assumed, I figured, that as I had tattoos too, this book must be right for me. I have to admit, I never got through more than the first chapter before deciding that actually it wasn't for me. The movie looked decent though, and Sarah and I eagerly waited for it to start. At this point I should mention that Sarah comes from a very religious family; she rarely drinks and doesn't (or didn't at the time) believe in sex before marriage. I am a card-carrying Atheist, but was largely a non-drinker, non-partyer and non-single at the time, and so our combined nanna-ness meant that we got on swimmingly due to these shared values (albeit for totally different reasons). Well, what we were greeted with within the first five or ten minutes of the film was enough to make both of us gag. Let's just say it was no rom-com. Rape, violence and masochism were the general themes of the movie, put to stunningly real effect by the filmmakers. I sat, eyes half closed for probably two thirds of the movie and relaxed only a little when finally the disgusting villain got his comeuppance with a beating of his own from the protagonist. I do enjoy a good, bloody, action film, but I can do without the rape and torture, thanksverymuch!

Stunned and silent, we eventually walked from the cinema. I told Sarah I needed something 'happy and normal' to shake me from my trauma-induced daze and so we did the happiest and most normal thing I could think of – we went to eat some more food. After a feast of shopping mall Mexican (don't knock it) I was ready to re-enter the world and we opted to take the car for a spin around the local suburbs of Manchester. We were not disappointed, as we soon stumbled across a housing estate that looked like something directly out of *Harry Potter*! We were both Harry fans, and could have sworn these streets were those same streets in Little Whinging where Harry and his cousin Dudley grew up. We took happy snaps while stealing furtive glances at house windows to make sure we weren't caught by any of the locals featuring their front lawns in our Potter-induced hysteria.

Happy with our afternoon's explorations and with the trauma of the awful movie behind us, we retired for the day in our hotel beds and rose again early the next morning for the next stage in our adventures.

On this day, we planned to drive up through the Lake District and on towards Edinburgh in Scotland. It would be a long drive, but we really didn't need to stop anywhere in between and so decided to make the trip in one slog. What we weren't prepared for was the absolute unmatched, straight-from-every-fantasy-novel-you've-ever-read scenery of the Lake District. Rolling green hills cascaded and met at tiny, stone bridges before crumbling into rocky, goat-spotted countryside. As we rounded one cobblestone-lined corner we came over yet another little rocky bridge and peered over the edge to see a stream bubbling and spattering below the bridge and up into the hills beyond. Sarah and I looked at one another with giant grins.

"It's a babbling brook, Sarah!"

"AN ACTUAL BABBLING BROOK," we both chimed, laughing maniacally together as we continued to weave through the country lanes. It was truly something out of a picture book. As we came upon a little English town also straight from a story, we decided we'd better stop for lunch. Tummies rumbling and eyes still wide from the sheer perfectness of our surrounds, we floated into a little yellow house that served as a restaurant and gift shop. We ordered pots of tea with scones, and soup-of-the-day to warm our bellies on this cold January day. As we slurped pumpkin soup and dolloped clotted cream onto scones we admired the crafts and handiworks that dotted the walls around us. Though I'm sure much of it was made in China, I was captivated by the little knick-knacks and curios that hung around us, with quirky quotes brandished on them such as *"life's too short to drink bad wine"* and *"good friends are like a good wine, they get better with age"*. I wanted to buy everything and stuff it in the boot of our Vauxhall. Luckily, Sarah was with me, and instead of letting me dwindle my savings by getting caught up in the moment, she most wisely reminded me of the already bulging sides of my suitcase, and the extra luggage fees I'd be paying at the airport if I wasn't careful. We finished our tea, soup and scones and made our way from the little yellow house and out into the cool air. The sun struggled to peek through the ever-present clouds and the effect was, like everything else in this perfect little town, movie-like. We wandered the cobbled streets just long enough to take some touristy, artsy, *look-at-me-walking-down-the-lane-all-deep-in-thought* type photos and peek into the picture-perfect pubs as we made our way back to our car.

Fookin' Falkirk (Scotland)

Onwards we headed, as the day grew late and shadows stretched out in front of us. The sun dipped behind the hills as we rolled through the countryside in our car. By four o'clock is was totally dark and beginning to sleet. I drove ever-slower as the street lights petered out and we left behind the tiny towns for the vast expanses and farming land that join the north of England with the south of Scotland. I was only doing about 30 miles per hour as I made my way slowly over a dark hill, Sarah dozing off beside me. Too late, I realised that I'd just sailed through an unlit and unsigned intersection. Within a split second, a car appeared from the darkness to my right and came shooting out in front of the Vauxhall. I hit the brakes, although not too hard as the roads were awash with sleet and ice. I managed to slow the car without fish-tailing or losing control. However ,I clipped the taillight of the Honda Jazz that had swept past me in the millisecond before I braked.

The little car spun out; round and round it went and off the road into the grass beyond. I came to a stop in the middle of the intersection, facing north, engine still running. I quickly took a panicked look across at Sarah. I'd instinctively thrown my left arm out across her as we'd hit, and now I could see that she was shocked, mouth open but otherwise fine. She confirmed this, and I pulled the car across the intersection and into the car lot on the other side of the road. Of course, out here, in the wilderness between England and Scotland, of all the places I could have had a car accident, it had to be right outside a pub. I didn't know whether to be thankful or to cry. Several heads poked out from pub windows and a couple of bodies bounded down

141

to see what the fuss was about. After parking the car safely, I ran across the road to check whether the other driver was ok. Still in her car and obviously a little shaken, the small middle-aged woman inside assured me that she was ok, just rattled. The publican made his way out to the car and with a warm and concerned greeting asked us all inside and out of the cold. Sarah, the other driver and I all made our way into his pub while he rang the police for us. After several more apologies to Harriet (the Honda driver), I rang the insurance agency for the rental car and was asked to assess the damage on our car. As only a headlight had been smashed and very little else was damaged, we were told that we could continue on our trip as planned, so long as the car was drivable, and that the depot where we were due to drop the car off in a few days would take care of everything. Relieved somewhat, I put down the phone and continued to apologise to Harriet and to Sarah, and thanked the publican repeatedly for his cups of tea and concern for us all. I could have certainly done with something a little stronger than tea, but we still had a couple of hours driving ahead of us.

In time, the local police officer arrived and gave each of the cars a once-over, assessing that Harriet's car would be fine and simply needed a new rear taillight and possibly bumper. After exchanging details and assuring her that I was fully covered by insurance, we made our way back to the car and were on our way again.

"Sarah ..." I said, once we were a few minutes into the journey again, "let's not tell your parents about this one until we get home, ok? I don't need them thinking I just nearly killed their youngest daughter. I couldn't live with myself."

Laughing, she agreed. She was unfazed once she had shaken off the initial shock. Harriet had clearly been speeding, although the accident was entirely my fault. Sarah's parents were two of the nicest people I'd ever met and I considered them somewhat surrogate parents. I knew they'd just worry and fret and wonder if we were ok, but I really didn't want to face that kind of concerned scrutiny until I'd had time to process the accident in my own head and come to terms with it. Somewhat more wary of sudden and unsigned intersections, we made our way to our Edinburgh destination.

Car accident aside, Scotland was more than I had ever dreamed it would be. The beauty of the Lake District was surpassed only by the medieval, rugged country-side of greater Edinburgh and finally by the magnificent Edinburgh Castle. I was still feeling a little shell-shocked and guilty after the events of the night when we checked out the town the next day. Soon though, the beauty of the city and its cobblestone streets shook the monkey off my back and I was basking in yet more blissful story-book scenery. We chatted to locals at the village market and explored the surrounds of the castle. At one stage, I drove up a one-way street which, like most things in Scotland, was poorly signed, and found myself face to face (or bumper) with an outer wall of the castle. Nobody on foot seemed to mind or pay us the slightest atten-tion and so I figured that it must happen quite a bit. I parked the car back down the street, and we decided our explorations would be best spent on foot until we were ready to leave that day. We strolled through laneways and into gift stores, purchasing a few essentials (gaudy fridge magnets and whimsical coasters for me; cards and CDs for Sarah), and skipped up and down meandering staircases and alleys to yet more streets of giftware shops, cafes and teahouses. Every local we met was genuinely friendly and helpful, quick to give a smile or lend a hand when we needed directions. Although hard to understand, their accents are one of my favourite in the world. They spoke so quickly and with such enthusiasm that Edinburgh was quickly becoming one of my favourite cities.

Sightseeing-exhausted, we decided it was time to head off. Although I could have spent a week or more in Edinburgh just soaking up the beautiful city, we had an important mission to complete. We'd found some insanely cheap flights from Glasgow to Dublin online (only £14!) and although they weren't until the next morning, we'd been given a quest by my dad which needed to be completed on the way to Glasgow. Time was of the essence if we were to make it!

Dad had always wanted to go to Scotland, as he believed we have Scottish heritage (ask my mum and she'll say it's Irish. Harsh rivalries there, perhaps that's what led to their divorce when I was just a babe). Jacqui, my stepmum had wanted to take Dad to Scotland, but a couple of months earlier he'd been diagnosed with cancer. At this stage we didn't know just what a toll it would take only a couple of years later, but his chances of making it to Scotland were dwindling and there was one sight he was dying to see. Dad, being an engineer of sorts (left school early, became apprentice mechanic and eventually fully-fledged genius engineering Rain Man), was fascinated by the contraption called the Falkirk Wheel. I'd never heard of the thing, but was assured by Dad that it was a feat of engineering mastery and could not be missed. I was happy to accept the challenge, if only to bring him back a gaudy fridge magnet of his own. And so, Sarah and I bundled up into the car and headed off in search of this amazing feat of industry.

When the GPS told us we'd made it to Falkirk, we weren't sure it wasn't telling porkies. There were no signs for this famous Falkirk Wheel and you could miss the town if you so much as blinked on your way by. I guess being a small area, it had that in its favour; we could roam the streets until we found it, as there weren't too many places it could be hiding. Eventually we came across a carpark at the end of a dusty road. There seemed to be some kind of information centre there, and we could see beyond it was a great big grey mass of steel. We couldn't make out what it was exactly, but we assumed that we must be in the right place as we'd exhausted all other options. For such an incredible attraction, there seemed to be very few other people around. With only one other car in the lot, I wasn't sure what to make of the place.

With nothing else for it, we entered the information building and were blasted by warm air, much to my delight (it was a typically freezing and windy day outside). The small, gift shop-esque room before us was crammed with stands selling magnets, egg-cups, beanies, among other things, the ever-present Scottish tea-towel. There was a lone woman manning the counter, and as we approached her she looked up from her magazine.

"Hello dears! Welcome to Falkirk!" She beamed the friendly smile, common to all of the Scots we'd met thus far.

"Umm, hi, how are you? We are looking for the … ah … Falkirk Wheel," I stumbled, utterly unsure of myself and worried that we were in the wrong place and would look like total fools.

"Yes, dears! It's right outside – just through those doors there, and you can see her! She's not operating today though – having some maintenance done – but if you come back tomorrow she'll be in action." I caught most of what she said a few seconds later, as my brain took a while to process the thick and fabulous accent. We made our way to the doors at the back of the room as she nodded and gestured that we were heading the right way. Back out into the blustery winter day we headed, and as my hair whipped and swirled in front of my face, I could make out a huge steel structure beyond the patio we stood on. Trying in vain to control my hair, I gasped as finally, I could make out its shape. The Wheel. The Falkirk Wheel.

Well. It sure was … massive. And grey. A great big grey, massive … thing! Apparently the Falkirk Wheel was a contraption (excuse me, engineers, for my poor explanation) which would raise canal boats from the lower canal to the higher one. Why on earth the river ... or canal ... was on two different levels, was totally beyond me. But this was it. This was my dad's number one bucket list tourist item, and now I was here. Sarah was as equally baffled by this bizarre tourist attraction as I was. If you could call it a tourist attraction, that is. Well, I guess, it did have its own gift shop and information centre. I suppose that made it a bona fide attraction.

Sarah took a photo of me standing in front of the giant wheel, freezing and pulling my jacket tight around me. I looked quite ridiculous and it summed up the weather that day just perfectly. I swiftly sent the photo to Dad via SMS with the caption, *"Falkirk Wheel! You bloody happy now? Haha!"*

We left the underwhelming attraction in search of more of a crowd pleaser: food. Back in town we found a smattering of pubs and cafes, and decided on one that sold craft beer and steak. Sarah, being a vegetarian and who rarely drank, was happy to order a meat-free something-or-other (I really don't remember) and I was thrilled to see a burrito on the menu. Our drinks were brought out by a burly Englishman who, before we'd even uttered a word, exclaimed, "You're from Australia!"

I don't know how people can always tell this before we've even spoken to them – perhaps we're loud enough for everyone to hear us coming!

"Yes!" we laughed, in response.

"Well," he grinned back, set our drinks down and scratched his head "What the *fook* are you doin' in Falkirk?"

We laughed until our stomachs hurt. Good question, buddy, loooong story!

12

Dun Where?

After an eventful trip through England and Scotland, Sarah and I were still travelling without plans beyond the next few hours at any given time. This was long before hostels in Paraguay, dodgy buses in Bolivia and other third-world adventures. This was my first taste of unscheduled travel, and I really enjoyed it. With our last-minute hire car and without so much as a hotel booking for that night, we'd gone to sit at McDonald's (to use their free wi-fi) to look up accommodation options for the next city. This became a regular habit over the next few days and, being winter in the UK, we never failed to bag a bargain hotel room.

So, when we absent-mindedly looked up the cost of flights to Dublin for later that week, we could hardly help but squeal when we realised we could fly there for only £14! We hastily booked a hotel room for our arrival in Temple Bar; the heart of Dublin's nightlife.

We arrived at the airport at a criminal hour on Friday morning. The airport check-in staff had not even arrived yet and we wondered why we'd bothered coming at the recommended time (according to the Ryanair website) when it turned out we had to wait another 45 minutes for the staff to arrive, mess around at their desks for an age and then have an chat with the rest of the staff, before finally calling forward the steadily building crowd. Our check-in was met with rash and abrasive service, and I remember being told off about several things before the check-in clerk would let us through with our boarding passes. Security was another silent panic while I waited (as I always do) for them to pull me aside and berate me about carrying some kind of deadly weapon like an umbrella, a plastic nail file or a tube of toothpaste. Finally, against all imaginary security threats, we made it through the rigmarole and in to the waiting area, sporting several layers of clothing and carrying a spare pair of shoes each, in order to avoid the exorbitant extra check-in bag fee. We sat together sweating in the small food court, despite the sub-zero temperatures outside and waited for our plane to arrive. It was delayed, and I would later learn that this is simply to be expected when flying with certain budget airlines (cough!).

Once finally onboard, after a walk across the tarmac in what felt like an arctic blizzard, we strapped ourselves in to our seats and tried not to think about the weather outside (and the fact that the plane was beginning to pitch from side to side). To our horror, once the cabin doors were locked and we were ready to take off, a woman in a nearby seat with a crying toddler rose and hurried up the aisle. There was some banter between the flight attendants and after merely seconds, the doors were reopened and the woman bundled her son down the stairs and across the tarmac towards the terminal. The doors were re-sealed and Sarah and I shot each other 'what the fuck?' looks, with barely concealed terror. The plane continued to rock from side to side, and the attendants busied themselves for takeoff.

It was only a 40-minute flight from Glasgow to Dublin and we assured ourselves that the Ryanair staff would be showing signs of trepidation if there was anything to worry about. This was the UK after all, and bad weather was part and parcel, part of the fun! (gulp!)

We took to the sky in a shaky and petrifying takeoff and soon were above the cloud lines. We weren't sure whether to even expect a drink service on such a short flight with a budget airline. However, soon the attendants were up and down the aisle spruiking everything from magazines, to cigarettes, to Ryanair merchandise and eventually, beverages. There were no less than four trips up and down the aisle before we began our descent. I was surprised, with all of the add-on costs and non-inclusions, that they hadn't charged us extra for the turbulence and for the privilege of having wings on the plane. At last we landed in an equally horrifying manner and were set free into the blisteringly cold Irish city of Dublin.

Although our coffers were dwindling steadily, this being the tail-end of our trip, we were in no mood to mess around with public transport and decided to catch a taxi to our hotel. The energetic cab driver spoke in hilarious and rapid Irish brogue and for a few moments we could barely understand him. There was the usual, 'where are you from' and 'how long are you here' business. We told him we'd be here for a couple of days and really didn't have too much planned.

'Well loves, you can skip the fookin' Guinness factory. They'll charge ye 15 Euro for a tour, and ye doon even git a beer wit dat! Best to head to yer nearest poob and buy yerself two pints eh Guinness and 'ave yerself a better experience for de same proice!'

We laughed and cajoled for the rest of the ride, before he dropped us outside the hotel with a big wave and grin, and best wishes for our stay in his city. We barrelled ourselves through the door to reception and tried to plaster *'please help us we're cold and tired and I promise we're friendly'* looks on our faces as we approached the desk hoping to check into our rooms a full five hours early. We'd never had any trouble in Scotland with this, and we'd come to expect charming and helpful service from any hotel we encountered. It was not to be so, here in Temple Bar. The receptionist was less than impressed with our pained-but-friendly expressions, and told us that check-in wasn't until two o'clock. She didn't even offer us a seat in the waiting area. We enquired as to what we might do with our bags while we tried to find something to do for the next five hours, and she begrudgingly took them behind the counter to hold until our return. We scanned the notice board for maps and local city guides, wondering where we might be able to spend a few hours in Dublin in the wee hours of the morning. Ever unhelpful, the receptionist didn't recommend anywhere and so we decided to simply go for a stroll.

Re-donning our scarves and several layers of cloth-ing, we headed out to brave the city. We soon came upon a teahouse called the Queen of Tarts and rushed inside into the warmth. To our disappointment there was no roaring open fireplace to sit next to, however it was dry and warm and, most importantly, had comfy seats. Perhaps more importantly, it had tea. Lots of tea. And cakes. Lots and lots of cakes. We found a quiet corner and drank cup after cup of Earl Grey out of teapots with hand-crocheted tea cosies in varying shades of eccentric. We ate cakes and tarts and scones lumped with clotted cream and jam and we had a pretty good time of it. I may have dozed off once or twice against the wall, and used the cushions dotted around the room to build myself a bit of a cushion fort. Before we knew it, we'd killed four hours. We settled our bill and headed back down the street to the hotel, hoping that she might let us in now that it was after 1:00 pm. No joy. She pointed us towards the waiting area and so, with nothing else for it, we took a seat.

We languished there for a few minutes drifting in and out of exhaustion-induced couch comas, while other guests started to arrive downstairs for departure. We shot hopeful glances at the receptionist each time someone checked out, on the chance that this might mean our room was available. No such luck for a while. While sitting there sporting an ever increasing disdain for the receptionist, her family and her future spawn, I noticed another patron waiting across the room. He was studiously working away on his laptop, typing something up and consulting what I supposed was a guide book periodically. He looked up just as I glanced towards him again, and too fatigued to turn away quickly, I simply gave him a 'what can ya do?' shrug and smiled benignly. He grinned and mouthed 'You look how I feel.' Well great, I thought. I am clearly dishevelled and in need of a shower and a bed right now, but thanks for pointing it out. I smiled back at him and actually started to laugh. I was beyond the point of shattered.

We all sat quietly for a few more minutes before it finally ticked over to 2:00 pm and I couldn't take it anymore. I approached the desk in one last attempt to gain access to our room before I gave up and slept on the floor in protest. Thank all that is good in this world, she finally smiled in false affability and handed over my key. Sarah whooped audibly and we gathered up our bags, gave a, 'hey, you're up next!' nod to the man in the corner and headed for the lift. Except there was no lift. In this pre-war building, there was only a staircase for all five flights up to our room. We almost couldn't bear it. Only the promise of a bed, a hot shower and lack of plans to emerge for the rest of the day prevented us from throwing a tandem toddler-like tantrum right there on the hand-woven rug. Agonisingly, we dragged our bags up all five flights, crawled down the hallway, crashed through our door and immediately onto our lumpy twin beds. We didn't move for several hours.

Bleary-eyed, I emerged from my slumber to a dark room and only the faint sound of Sarah's breathing (thankfully Sarah was not a snorer). I tripped and stumbled over to the window and pulled back the curtains. It was well and truly dark outside, and the streetlights below were blazing in a charming turn-of-the-century oil-lantern type of way that reminded me of *The Lion, The Witch and the Wardrobe*. Sarah groaned and grumbled and peered out from behind her covers.

"What time is it?" she asked.

I checked my watch, "It's 7:00 pm. Dinner time!"

She pulled herself from her bed and after both of us had rustled through our bags to find some sort of cosmetics, brushes and hair spray, we emerged from the room looking at least slightly more presentable than we had a few hours ago. We were feeling much better with some sleep under our belts. However, we climbed down the stairs like a couple of zombies in search of some sustenance. We didn't even bother to approach the night-staff at the desk for a dinner recommendation and we stood for a few minutes consulting our smartphones for a possible nearby eatery. Preferably a pub. Just as we were deciding between several promising establishments in the area, the '*you look how I feel*' man appeared from the stairwell. He was looking decidedly chirpier too and bounded over to us.

"You two get some sleep?" He was American. Tall and pale and wearing a pair of reading glasses, he looked friendly and non-threatening. "I'm Jason."

"Haha, yes, we did, thank goodness. But now we need some FOOD!" I explained, while Sarah diligently stared at her phone. She was not really in the mood to socialise with strangers, and didn't possess that irrational need to always appear overly polite and accommodating like I did.

"Ah, yes, me too," said Jason. "I have been really looking forward to trying this vegan restaurant around the corner. It's in my guidebook and it's meant to be great!"

That did the trick for Sarah. Hearing the word 'vegan' I could almost see her ears pull back in anticipation as she looked up from her phone. Sarah was a vegetarian and always had trouble finding good vegetarian options anywhere in Europe. She had been to Europe before and even lived in the UK for six months the year before, and was fairly resigned to the meagre offerings she could expect. When we were in Paris, she'd asked for a 'vegetarian breakfast' at a café and been presented with a plate of wet spinach leaves.

With the decision made by the growl in our stomachs and Sarah's obvious glee at having found a fellow vegan-appreciator, we headed out into the night. Walking the cold streets of Dublin was like a dream come true. We passed frosty pub windows, with fires crackling away inside and trendy young Irishmen and women drinking, laughing and chatting. The wide, cobbled streets twisted and turned as we followed Jason's guidebook and Sarah's nose to the restaurant. When we arrived a few minutes later I had my reservations about the place. With its too-white walls and its sparsely decorated tables, it looked like expensive snobbery to me. I would have happily devoured a steak and Guinness pie and chips for dinner, but it was not to be. Sarah looked ecstatic and I did have to admit, it smelled good. We bundled in out of the cold and were shown to a table by an efficient, well-dressed waiter. The menu offered such delicacies as parsnip soup; gluten, salt and butter-free garlic bread (taste-free more like it); vegan pizza and vegan chocolate cake. I settled on a pumpkin soup and vegan pizza and was actually surprised by how good it was, and how full I became. And all guilt-free!

Jason was friendly and funny, and we chatted easily and found ourselves laughing throughout our dinner together. He was an IT specialist from Portland, Oregon and was here to give a talk at Trinity College in a couple of days. He showed us photos of his wife and two young kids, Byrdie and Boomer. We were getting along marvellously, and despite Sarah's original trepidation for meeting and entertaining strangers, I could tell that she was also glad that we'd come across someone so friendly to spend some time with. We left the restaurant laughing and with full bellies, and headed back down the main street in search of a promising looking pub. It wasn't hard to find one, and soon we were removing our scarves and coats once again, and ordering drinks at a bar as a band began to start up. I ordered my very first pint of Guinness and waited excitedly for the bartender to pour it, leave it sitting half full, make several other drinks and then come back to finish it off. It took so long for the sediment to settle enough for the glass to be filled, it was like I was about to ingest a meat pie. Or several meat pies, more accurately. I carried it with both hands back to the small table we'd chosen and couldn't hide the grin on my face. The thing was bigger than my head, and I had Jason snap a photo of it next to my beaming face so that I could send it to Joel. Before I got his reply, "How the heck are you going to drink all of that, silly?" I was onto my second one.

We had a brilliant night there, listening to local band *The Statics* play their set and making our way through several beers each. By the time we made our way back to the hotel in the wee hours, we were all on a high and utterly tuckered out.

"Hey girls, what have you got planned for tomorrow?" Jason asked as he started to climb the stairs.

We had nothing in particular planned, but wanted to see some of the Irish countryside, we told him.

"My guidebook tells me that I should visit the seaside town of Dun Laoghaire while I'm here. It's an historical port town and meant to be worth a look. Want to come on the train with me?"

In my happy Guinness-fuelled stupor, I could not have been keener. Sarah was up for it as well. We agreed in unison and organised to meet downstairs in the morning at 10:00 am. We then clambered up the stairs loudly and clumsily and made our way to our glorious, glorious lumpy mattresses. I slept like a baby that night. Albeit a drunk and reeking-of-beer baby. We rose the next morning at 9:30 am and, having had two good sleeps to our name in the last 24 hours, we were feeling chipper. Excited for our Irish seaside town adventure today, we showered and readied ourselves before making our way downstairs.

Jason was waiting there, reading his guidebook once again. It seems he'd found this book to be the authority on all things Irish and it rarely left his side. We grinned and hugged and headed out into the town to find a quick breakfast and head to the train station. Far from the rustic historical look that the rest of Dublin's features seemed to sport, the train station and the trains themselves were modern, gleaming and decidedly 21st century. Jason helped us to buy tickets (we still had a bit of trouble with pronouncing Dun Laoghaire) and before too long we boarded our train.

As we sat alone in our carriage, we swapped stories of home and our families and what had brought us to Ireland. I told Jason about my dad, and about his request for me to see the Falkirk Wheel while I was in Scotland. I told him how my dad would build hydraulic-powered mammoth steel constructions in his giant man-shed and then explain to me how each of its parts worked while I looked on in earnest and without the faintest hint of understanding.

"He sounds like a great man," Jason said, after listening intently with a fatherly smile on his face. "I am sure he'd be very proud of you. I hope my kids talk about me the way that you talk about your dad when they're older."

"I'm sure they will, Jason," I grinned back at him. Talking about my dad always made me smile and get carried away; talking about his brilliance and my obvious envy of his intellect and general amazingness.

He'd only been diagnosed a few months before I left on my trip to Europe. I was at a work conference in Sydney when Jacqui called me and told me the news. He'd been told that he probably had bladder cancer, but that they needed to do a biopsy or some such to work out whether or not it was contained or had spread to the outer lining and even more awfully, the rest of his organs. We didn't know much at this stage, Jacqui told me, and they were hopeful that they'd caught it early. I remember being dumbfounded as she spoke. It felt as though I'd been winded. I was standing on my balcony, overlooking Sydney Harbour in the distance. Clouds rolled in and it started to rain lightly as I slumped to the tiles, too shocked and dazed to notice that the rain was blowing in and over me. I wished I could have offered more supportive, encouraging 'he's going to be fine' type words of comfort to Jacqui, but it all seemed so fake and futile. I wanted to leave right then, to get on a plane and head home and race to their house. There was no point though; it would be another week before his tests, and he was in good spirits for now, she told me. I doubted that was true, but Jacqui was Dutch and typically stoic. And Dad was Dad. Strong and fiercely intelligent. Tough and rugged and callous-fingered and infallible. He was a heavy smoker from the age of 12, and I had always known in that innate way that you know your parents will die before you but you don't want to admit, that he would succumb to some kind of smoker's disease. Lung cancer. Emphysema. But bladder cancer? It seemed so cruel and random and unrelated.

I did all that I could do in that moment and went into problem-solver research mode. When had they found out? What had they already tested for? What was the doctor's initial prognosis? What were his options when they found out the next results? What was the most likely scenario? Jacqui didn't have a lot of answers yet, but she had told me what she could. I told her I loved her and hung up the phone. I held back the tears that threatened to cascade, and opened my computer. I searched for figures and survival rates and treatment programs and just gobbled up any information I could find in the magical pages of Dr Google. I found comfort in statistics, my analytical brain made jumps to lottery odds and horse-racing. There were several ways to sway the odds in your favour, and I'd take 50 per cent odds in a lottery sweepstakes any day. He's going to be fine, I thought. He's going to be fine. He's going to be fine. He's going to be fine.

* * * *

The train rolled along the coastline as Jason, Sarah and I talked and stared out the windows. It was a bleary day, not raining but cloudy and cold and breezy. It was typically Irish, I thought to myself. I'd dreamed of coming here ever since I could remember. My mum had fostered a love of our Irish heritage in me, and although she knew virtually nothing about our ancestors, she was certain that they'd been Irish and that Ireland was in our blood. I didn't speak to my mother much anymore, but I couldn't deny the impact that these beliefs had had on me. I watched the coastline fly by as the waves broke on rocky cliffs and pebbly beaches shivered with sea spray and the roar of the wind. It felt good to be here, and it felt like home in a way that no French or Bavarian or Dutch town had done.

We finally arrived at our station and stood for a few moments on the platform wondering what next? Jason consulted his guidebook once again, and we decided we'd make our way down to the beach first before heading into Dun Laoghaire proper for some lunch and sightseeing. I'd lived on the Gold Coast for years by now, where some of the most beautiful beaches in the world were visited year-round for surfing and sunbaking. Where we next found ourselves, I would not so much describe as a beach, but as a broad strip of pebbles which happened to meet the wintry Irish Sea. The sand was dark and flaky, like so many trillion grey shells all but ground down into tiny scales and scattered across the coastline. Large quartz pebbles littered the beach too, and I bent down to collect a few of the more beautiful and interesting ones. Although I hadn't spoken to Mum in months, I wanted to take a few of these home for her. I imagined her placing them on the window sill above the sink, or in a jar on her kitchen table and thought of her smiling and wishing she could be on this very beach collecting pebbles for herself.

We took photos there, rugged up in our coats, thick scarves and gloves with the rolling sea in the background. Sarah and I laughed and hugged and rubbed our arms as we shivered, loving every minute of our mini Irish adventure. We headed back up past the train station and into town, ready to see the sights of this historic village. We came across a park which sat close to the shore. There seemed to be a few locals out walking their dogs but otherwise the town was quiet. We strolled up Main Street in search of interesting Irish things to see but for once, Jason's guidebook fell short. There was really nothing to see here. The park and the beach seemed to be the main attractions, the portside town having long subsided into mundane suburbia. We made fun of Jason and his not-so-trusty guidebook as it started to rain, and ran from boutique shop to shop in search of something memorable to buy. Apart from overpriced gaudy handbags and dress jewellery, there was nothing much of interest and so we defaulted to our recreational activity of choice; beer in a pub. Preferably with a fireplace.

It was still early – not yet midday – and we finally found the local watering hole nestled further up Main Street. We looked longingly through the windows for a fireplace, but were disappointed. Still, it looked rustic and postcard-esque enough, and so we entered and looked for a place to sit. A burly barmaid stood behind the counter and eyed us warily as we made our way to a table. She didn't bother to break herself away from what I assume was an animated conversation with the sole other patron about 'the youth of today' and how the town was 'going to the dogs', and so I made my way to the bar to enquire about lunch.

"It ain't lunchtime til 12 o'clock!" she barked at me. It was quarter to 12 by now, and I explained to her that we'd be happy to wait with a beer until then.

She grudgingly poured me a Guinness and I ordered a coke and a cider for Sarah and Jason. She wouldn't let me place an order until she was good and ready after 12 o'clock. So we waited, patiently sipping our drinks at our table by the window. The weather worsened outside and I wished silently that we'd taken a train inland to the rolling green hills and craggy highlands that I imagined were waiting for me further to the West. Every movie I'd seen and book I'd read about Ireland had always been full of details of emerald hills, sheep, winding country lanes and leprechauns. I had never pictured the coast or this quiet, suburban coastal town when I'd imagined myself here on the Emerald Isle. Still, I was here with good people and with Guinness and would soon console myself with a glorious steak and Guinness pie; and that had to count for something.

The waitress finally agreed to take our orders when I made my way back over to the bar at midday.

"No steak and Guinness pie today!" she shrieked. "Today it's chicken curry!"

We ordered chicken curry pies and chips (Sarah just had chips), and more beers. We sat there in the little Irish pub in that little Irish seaside town and watched the rain dribble down the windows as we whiled away the afternoon. Looking back on it now, that sounds wonderful. In hindsight, it was.

The next day we said goodbye to Dun Laoghaire, to Ireland and to Jason, heading back to London for a final few days before our European adventure was over.

13

Where's My Cucumber?
... and Other Air Travel Mishaps

As I've already mentioned, I was scared of flying before I'd ever set foot on a plane. However, since that first flight to Bali in 2005, I have flown countless times for both work and for pleasure. While I've largely managed to tone-down my turbulence-induced panic attacks, there are plenty of other interesting experiences that you can have on planes. You really just never know what you're going to encounter when you board through that gate.

Here are just four episodes of my AIR TRAVEL ADVENTURES:

1. FIRST FLIGHT

You've already heard about my fear of everything, and that flying was no exception to this in my earlier years. On the flight home from Bali, I was no less scared than I was on the outbound journey. However, I refrained from drawing the blood of poor Cheri this time, and contented myself with silent screams and protests against the turbulence. Props to me for silent and stoic panic!

The in-flight meal on this particular flight was an ambiguous choice of 'chicken' or 'fish'. I figured it was safer to go with the chicken. It was the lesser of two salmonella-prone proteins I suppose, and who knew what other ghastly intestinal maladies the 'fish' could contain!

My 'chicken' dish turned out to be some kind of curry with plain white rice. Perfect! I chomped away greedily, only to discover a tiny piece of stray capsicum in my rice. Whatever, I love capsicum, no biggie. Chomp. Only it wasn't capsicum. It was chili. *Red hot, burn-a-giant-hole-in-your-mouth chili.* Holy Jesus! Some embarrassing hand gestures and miming with the stewardess eventually resulted in a glass of milk for me to drink and sooth my insides briefly.

When I returned to Australia, I was determined to become more 'worldly' and to develop my tastes for hot food. I had dinner with some friends at a Thai restaurant (close enough to Indonesian, right?) and did the 'I've just been to Bali; I've got this' look, ordered a green chicken curry and then surreptitiously asked the waitress to make it mild. 'No,' I said to her, 'stupidly, stupidly Australian mild.' Baby steps, yeah? The waitress nodded encouragingly, and scuttled away with our orders.

I can only assume that the wait staff and kitchen had a running joke on their idiot Australian patrons, as what came out on my plate could not in my dizziest daydreams ever, EVER be deemed remotely mild. The thing was NAPALM! I swear, I could barely speak. I gesticulated wildly for the waitress and requested a cucumber. 'A whole cucumber?' She looked confused.

"A whole damn cucumber. Bring me a cucumber! PLEASE!"

I don't know what exactly she thought I was going to get up to with that cucumber, but what arrived was a totally unhelpful glass of milk.

2. PANIC ATTACKS AND BAD FLYERS (not me for once!)

So, you thought I was a bad flyer? The Bali episode was the first of many flights I would take over the coming years, and while I wouldn't exactly say I enjoy it these days, I have certainly come a long way.

Never was this more apparent than when I recently took a trip from Cairns to Brisbane for work. When I sat down in seat 3A (right behind the business class section, I could ALMOST feel the smugness emanating from the seats just beyond the partition), I thought I'd scored when, as the plane filled up, no one came to claim the seats next to me. Time to relax and spread out? No such luck. Hustling and bustling their way on, the last two (late) passengers arrived and parked themselves in 3B and 3C.

I returned, unperturbed, to my book and continued reading. Shortly a tap, tap on my arm.

"I just have to let you know," said 3B, "I am a really bad flyer."

3C piped up, "Tell her what you're really like. She has to sit next to you for two hours!"

"Ok," said 3B, "I'm really, really bad. Like, I sometimes scream." Oh joy!

"That's no problem," I said, empathetically. "I am a terrible flyer too. I'm sure you're no worse than me."

We sat for the obligatory waiting around, and eventually the plane started to taxi. 3B and 3C were happily chatting away – two old girlfriends who were obviously on a girls' weekend trip together. As we started to speed up, suddenly 3B stopped mid-conversation and went completely silent. Chancing a glance over, I saw her sitting bolt upright against her chair, hands clenched on each arm rest (I told her she was welcome to mine earlier) and eyes firmly shut. Poor poppet!

Then the groaning started. Oh dear! I don't know what the people around us thought was going on exactly, but it was certainly entertaining – guttural noises emanating from the little woman beside me, tears starting to find their way down her cheeks. Her companion seemed uninterested, reading her magazine and largely ignoring poor 3B. Perhaps this was some tough love? Perhaps trying to soothe her only made it worse? But I couldn't just sit there. Not only did I feel awful for her (after all, I knew what it was like to be petrified on a flight!) but the noises she was making were beginning to really rouse the interest of our fellow passengers. I patted her on the shoulder and held her arm, 'It's ok, we're nearly up. Just a bit of turbulence on takeoff, but it'll be over soon.' This was met with appreciative grunts, but 3B was certainly under the assumption that if she removed her hands from the arm rests or opened her eyes for even a second, the plane would surely crash.

3C steadfastly refused to show an ounce of sympathy and continued to read her *New Idea* mag. Finally, mercifully, the plane levelled out and the beverage trolley began to make the rounds. Having at last decided that the safety of the flight was not directly linked to the strength with which she could hang onto the arm rests, 3B peeled away her clutches and searched for her wallet. As the drinks trolley reached our row, she (a little too enthusiastically) ordered herself three scotches. Neat. She threw each one back with vigour and sighed audibly as the magic amber liquid must have slithered like treacle down her panic-dry throat. She seemed to relax and decide that perhaps we weren't all going to die after all. 3C even deigned to resume friendly conversation once again and all was well in the world. Despite the occasional crying baby, the rest of the flight whizzed by without incident.

Until the pilot announced that we were starting our descent.

I won't bore you with the details. Literally read the last couple of paragraphs in reverse and that's basically how the whole ordeal went down. Not until we'd landed, taxied and at last come to a complete halt did she finally give it a rest. Drenched in sweat, hair frazzled and puffy-eyed – I've never seen someone so relieved to exit a plane.

Whenever I have a tiny little flash-back to my extreme-flying-paranoia days, I just remember poor 3B and content myself that I've made some impressive progress.

3. BUSINESS CLASS ROOKIES

My next international flight was in 2011 – a good six years since I'd flown with Cheri to Bali. I was flying to London, via Abu Dhabi with my girlfriend Sarah. Sarah had a bit of flying experience and international travel under her belt and to date, my experience hadn't extended beyond Indonesia. Needless to say, I was intensely excited, albeit a bit daunted to be catching a 14-hour first leg to the other side of the world. Despite my trepidation, I couldn't contain my exhilaration at the prospect of the incredible four-week journey that lay ahead of us, and we approached the check-in desk practically jumping out of our skins.

While we waited for a free counter at check-in, we busied ourselves with excited chit-chat and ogled at the other guests checking in. There were lots of exotic-looking couples and rowdy 2.5 kid families. I wondered, day-dreamily about where each of them was headed, where they were from and, most importantly, how much flying experience they had. Play it cool, Mags. Act like you know how this works. Flying to London? Oh yes, darling, no big deal!

The line was moving slowly, and as we were at the head of it we watched with some curiosity (nosiness, more like) as the woman checking in at the nearest desk seemed to be making a bit of a nuisance of herself. She was about 150 years old (at least) and seemed to repeatedly rush (as much as a one-hundred-and-fifty-year-old person can rush) back to the frazzled ground crew member at the desk and berate him about something or other. This went on for an amusing (bemusing) 10 or 15 minutes before she finally seemed satisfied enough to walk away from the desk, boarding pass in hand.

The chap at the desk in question called us forward and we lugged our bags, haphazardly across the floor and presented them – smiles abounding. We had our documents and passports ready with a flourish, and the guy behind the desk was clearly relieved to have perfectly contented guests to deal with on this occasion. We made idle chit-chat as he typed away on the computer; until he came to a stop, looking down at my passport and looked puzzled. Oh fucking fuck fuck. Fuck it! My maiden name before I was married was McDonald. As you can imagine, dear reader, as unless you're a McDonald yourself you've probably done it too – the travel agent had booked me as a *MacDonald* on the tickets. Fuck! This usually never poses a problem, as anyone with half a brain can match my name and date of birth to my identification and infer that, as usual, it is merely an error on behalf of the booking agent and a simple typing mistake. This was no ordinary trans-action, though. This was international travel. Long-haul flights. Visas. Passports. Documents upon documents and regulations upon regulations. Fucking fuck!

"I just need to make a quick call," the bloke explained. Without any hint of expression, he picked up the phone and began to speak in airport-code-or-some-thing to whoever was on the other end of the line. Sarah and I exchanged mild expressions of panic. I gave her some sort of encouragement along the lines of, 'Save your-self. Go without me. I'm done for.'

Meanwhile, our mate behind the desk continued to speak in code. "I need a 1-5-7 on the APG for a D11 and an F2100. Yep. Yep. Nope. Ok."

He hung up the phone. I held my breath. Sarah gripped my arm. A little bit of wee came out. He turned slowly back to us; stony-faced.

"So …" he began. Oh. My. God. This moment seemed to last foreverrrrr. What, man? Give me the diagnosis!

"You guys are going to *LUUUUUURVE* me!" he did his best Peter Allen impression.

We exchanged bewildered looks. We couldn't yet manage speech and so just stared with open mouths at the bloke. "So. I have … just upgraded you … to *BUSINESS CLASS*!" he cried, still doing Peter Allen.

We instantly lost our shit. Squealing, jumping and hugging each other. This lasted for several ecstatic seconds before we collected ourselves, straightened our shirts and composed our expressions. Wait a minute, I thought. I don't even have a clue what that means, in reality. I told him as much.

He started to explain, before, "Just … just wait until you get there. You'll see!" He beamed, handing us our boarding passes and wishing us a happy flight.

Well! Waiting around for our flight to board, we busied ourselves with wild and imaginative speculation about what delights our exclusive new boarding passes would afford us beyond the gate. Huge seats? HUGE! Drinks? The best! Champagne? Of course!! Private toilet? Duh! Far out, surely the paparazzi will be arriving soon and little children will be asking for our autographs!

After what felt like forever, finally the flight was called for boarding. We weren't nearly savvy enough to realise that we had priority boarding, and so we waited around (with all of the other plebs) in line for the queue to shuffle forward, slowly. At last at the head of the queue, we were shown to our seats by the crew member in charge of boarding (who visibly adjusted her tone from the general, '*hullo*' uttered to regular passengers to the demonstrative, '*oh! Welllllcome aboard Miss McDonald and Miss Dyer! This waaaaay'* reserved for business class passengers. She was as shocked as we were that we were here!)

Being at the pointy end of the plane, (yipeee!) the walk to our seats wasn't a long one. Turn left (left!) and there we were; in snooty-class heaven. We were swiftly shown to our (enormous) seats and busied ourselves by checking out the contraptions and the excellent little array of flying paraphernalia (sleeping masks, folding tooth-brushes and tiny tubes of toothpaste, slippers, blankets and of course, cushions). Before long, the stewardess (or is the politically correct term 'flight attendant'? I am really not sure) had returned with our drinks menu. *Drinks menu!* (yipeee!)

With barely a moment to peruse (and still at this stage, not being much of a drinker) I quickly chose a variety of wine that looked as though I could drink it. I don't remember what it was called, but suffice it to say that I pronounced it wrong; and she corrected me. Whatever lady, I'm sitting in business class. I'll say it however I damn want! (Oh, how the power was going to my head!)

The other business class passengers were, I'm sure, not fooled for a moment about our inexperience in this part of the cabin. We made nuisances of ourselves by taking photos posing with our drinks, pretending to be asleep in our lie-flat-ish seats, and watching our headrest entertainment sets. I quickly pocketed the little satchel containing the mini-toothbrush and paste, as well as the eye mask and slippers. I definitely needed proof of this experience, and a few little souvenirs! (I actually still have the toothbrush and eye mask tucked away somewhere. Never throwing those out!)

Fear of flying, I learned that day, is dramatically reduced by the luxury and comfort of long-haul business class. The French onion soup, dinner rolls, stuffed chicken breast and crème brulee didn't hurt either. The rest of the flight passed in a euphoric blur. There couldn't have been a better way to start our epic adventure to Europe.

Subsequently, when I had to later fly home from Europe alone (Sarah was staying on to visit some relatives, and I had to get back to work), I tried a few tricks and put on my best smile in order to try and swing an upgrade for the trip home. No such luck, dang it!

4. FLYING AA (AEROLINEAS ARGENTINAS)

Long-haul flights are never fun unless you're in business class, as I now knew. Once more, I had no such luck for an upgrade when I flew home from Buenos Aires in 2013. After the ups and downs I'd had while backpacking for a month, I was truly ready to come home (and to hear some Aussie accents!), and I wasn't lucky enough to score a window seat on this solo voyage. I could just sense that this flight wasn't going to go my way. I did, however, score an aisle seat. I thought that this would at least afford me some space and privacy. Alas, it simply meant being repeatedly accosted by the drinks trolley, or by the elbows (or rather, the hind quarters) of passengers rushing to the toilets, which were right behind me. Stinky? Yes.

The young couple beside me looked to be first-time flyers judging by the way they had absolutely no idea of how things worked on board a plane. Late to find their seats (again, I thought I was going to score a free row!), no plane etiquette, but for the most part they were quiet and (damn them, how did they do it?) sleeping; when they weren't making-out mercilessly within inches of my protesting ears. I have never mastered the art of sleeping on planes, and so I simply plugged in my headphones and tried to ignore the slurping and sucking going on beside me.

My phone was nearly flat after hours of music playing, when we came into that glorious last two hours of the flight and the captain announced that we'd soon be able to see land. (Woo!) It was then that things took a turn for the worse in the seats next to me. Miss First-Timer was not dealing well with the turbulence (I hear you, love!) and proceeded to fill her sick bag ... as well as Mr First-Timer's sick bag ... and then mine, when I offered it.

I wasn't out of practice in the stomach-evacuating department, as I'd recently had my own travel-induced tummy upset. On my first morning in Peru, I'd wandered around the capital city in search of some breakfast nosh and had eventually settled in a dimly lit but beautiful upstairs café. I'd ordered the full works (well, as full a works as you can get in most of South America) which consisted of some scrambled eggs, some limp buttered toast, a strange assortment of fruit slices, a glass of juice and a coffee. Within moments of my first bite, I felt that all-too-familiar grumbling in my stomach and the telltale watering of my mouth. Oh no. Oh no. *Oh no Oh no Oh no!* I knew I had only moments to spare. I was upstairs, and I hadn't seen a bathroom on my way in. Despite my Spanish being terrible, I did thankfully know the word for bathroom. I practically ran around the restaurant trying to find the sole staff member on hand.

"*Banyo, banyo, banyo?*" I garbled. She paled. And pointed down the stairs.

Oh for fucks' sake! Of course it would be down the stairs. Seconds to spare. Seconds! I raced down the stairs like an Olympic stair-runner, and frantically (and comically, I'm sure) flung myself from door to door looking for the universal little picture signifying 'ladies room'. Finally, I found it.

Insides churning, buttocks and jaw firmly clenched, I burst through the doors without a glance at the other stalls and had to make a split-second decision: butt or face first? My stomach made the decision for me, and I projectile vomited in the general direction of the toilet bowl, horror-movie style. No sooner had the contents of my stomach exhausted themselves than my bowel screamed for a round of toilet-bingo. Butt down, with not a moment to spare, I spent the next several minutes with head in hands, trying not to throw up all over my clamped knees.

Body successfully expelled of demons, I slowly sauntered back up the stairs to my now-cold breakfast, looking like a recovering addict; all shaky and sweaty and glassy-eyed. Try as I might, I couldn't stomach another mouthful and so I simply paid and left. I searched for the dime-a-dozen pharmacy and prepared myself for the sign language/mime routine that I would have to follow in order to explain my condition to the attendant in order to procure the appropriate medication. The pharmacist watched, smiling politely as I gestured to my mouth and made arching-vomit-hitting-floor type moves. She gestured to her stomach, pushed it out and rubbed it in a bun-in-the-oven impression. No, no, no I assured her; not pregnant! Just sick! Turns out the Spanish word for nausea is 'nausea'; only pronounced as though you're a deaf person or someone who's just learning to read. I articulated it as best I could and she seemed to understand, for she left and soon returned with a sheet of little white pills. As they sell them by the pill, I asked for four (hoping it was just a short-lived tummy upset), paid and left.

I had a flight leaving in just a few hours, and so I hailed a cab from my hostel, took a couple of the pills and then eventually sat at the airport gate, awaiting my flight. Within minutes, I was completely conked out right there in the waiting area, completely knocked-out by the little white pills. When I finally awoke, it turned out that my gate had changed and I was practically alone. I frantically rushed around the airport, still foggy-headed and mercifully found my gate within minutes of the boarding closing. Thankfully, the pills seemed to do the trick for my stomach and I had no further issues with it. Yikes!

Back on the AA flight back to Sydney, Miss First-Time-Flyer was still hurling her guts up into any sick bag on offer. She and Mr First-Timer didn't speak a word of English, so after several entertaining minutes of mime (probably not so entertaining for her, I realise in hindsight), young Miss understood that I was trying to offer her the last of my mysterious anti-nausea medication. She took the pills gratefully and tried not to throw up for the thirty-seventh time. I held my breath until we finally landed.

Flying is an adventure in itself ... really!

14

Saying Goodbye
(Peru)

Of all the mishaps I'd encountered (and avoided) in
South America, perhaps none were as hair-raising as the encounter with bag-searching officials
at the Cusco International Terminal, in Peru. I'm not the
type to smuggle contraband; nonetheless, airport officials
make me break out in a sweat on the best of days. I'd
enjoyed such a lack of interest in my baggage (not so much
as a sniff from a friendly explosives-detective dog), I had
become quite used to the idea of sailing through customs
without a care. However, when I breezed across the terminal building that final day in Peru, due for my outbound
flight to Argentina and then home, I almost had a heart
attack; they were searching bags at the check-in desk.
Fuck!

Why was I so worried, you might well ask? Well,
you see … I'd carried my dad's ashes with me all through
South America. I'd been through the length of Argentina,
Paraguay and Bolivia by bus, and over into Peru via a few
eventful plane rides. All the while, I'd had my dad's ashes

hidden in a makeup container stashed deep inside my back-pack where I hoped it wouldn't be discovered by border officials, stray animals or thieves. What thieves would want with a makeup jar full of human remains, I couldn't rightly say, but it was precious cargo to me, and this made me wary. Not to mention the illicit nature of my smuggled goods. The transportation of human ashes required all sorts of paperwork, back-and-forth and rigorous screen-ing processes between each of the visited countries and the Department of Foreign Affairs and Trade (DFAT) back home in Australia. Not only had I left it too late to complete all of these prerequisites, I really wasn't entirely sure that they'd be accepted even if I'd complied with the regulations. The details and conditions of transportation of ashes were fairly nondescript and frankly, unhelpful on the DFAT website. However, it did seem to say that the transporting of ashes was far less frowned upon that the carriage of intact human remains across borders, and so I figured it was no harm – no foul.

I'd picked up 'Dad' on the Wednesday afternoon before I was due to leave home bound for Buenos Aires. His ashes had been waiting for collection at the funeral home for months now. It had been over a year since his death, and yet my step-mum Jacqui hadn't been able to bring herself to claim them. She'd had an awfully hard time of things since he'd died.

Jacqui and Dad had just finished building the house of their dreams on a patch of land south of Brisbane when he got sick. He was diagnosed before he'd had a chance to finish the back yard or landscape the garden beds that he'd planned for the front of the house. When it was clear that he was getting worse and that they'd have to sell the house, a collective of friends organised a working-bee to get the place finished and looking spick-and-span for the open homes that were sure to follow. Over 30 people arrived throughout the weekend and put their hands to everything from cleaning the rooms inside, to paving the driveway with stones, laying the garden beds and planting trees all around the drive. At one point, Jacqui pulled me aside and wondered aloud, "Why are all these people willing to spend their time doing this, in this heat, just to help us out?"

"Because you are good people. And this is what friends do for good people," was my reply. And it was true. They were the very best of people. Salt of the earth, and big-hearted. Dad was prone to offering his bobcatting services at a fraction of the quoted price, just to help out someone who'd struck up a good yarn with him and seemed as though they were in need of a break. He was gruff and often abrasive, but never turned down a request for a favour that he could afford (or often couldn't afford) to give.

People they'd only met once or twice turned up to that working-bee, having heard along the grapevine that Jacq and Greg needed help. Jacqui couldn't understand it, but I had no doubts about their motivations. This was just the kind of people they were, and good people attract good people, I thought. Simple as that.

The week before Dad's death, they'd signed the sale papers to their dream house and made an offer on a little three-bedroom brick home in a neighbouring suburb. It was certainly no match for the sprawling bungalow that he'd worked all of his life to be able to build, but Dad knew that his days were numbered and that he needed to leave his wife without the worry of a mortgage on top of everything else she'd have to deal with soon.

After a few months the 'grieving fatigue' started to hit their friends, and they slowly stopped coming around and checking in on Jacq. They didn't decide to stop caring, but gradually started to feel, as people do, that she was beginning to get over his death and move on with her life. She was far from it, in fact. But grief fatigue is well documented, and tends to move in after about three months. Now in her fifties and without much more to her name in the last 20 years but raising a son, maintaining a household and doing administration for Dad's business, Jacqui struggled to find work. Notwithstanding a high-flying career as a buyer for a leading department store in a previous life, her qualifications counted for little now that she was only a dozen years or so from retirement and re-entering the workforce. Applying for job after job after job and attending many interviews, she finally found work that paid barely enough to get her by. It took nearly 18 months. But it was a start.

When the time rolled around for me to prepare for my trip that week, I was thinking about Dad's ashes a lot. I really had wanted to do something special with them, and I knew that Jacqui did too. But what? We could scatter them over the ocean, in a tribute to his Fisherman Extraordinaire aspirations. But how clichéd would that be? We could turn him into a diamond, or some fireworks? Well, that would take time and money. So, a possibility, but unlikely.

On my last holiday, I'd taken an old photograph of Joel's face, taped it to a ruler and posed with it for cute and ridiculous photos in all sorts of exciting locations. In lieu of having him with me, I'd decided to take a caricature of him with me instead. It was hilarious, albeit a little bit creepy. It occurred to me that I could take Dad with me too! Rather than just a photo, which would surely make me tear up every time I pulled it from my bag, I could do something exciting, risky and more meaningful by taking his ashes with me and scattering them in incredible locations. It would add a touch of purpose to my trip, make it more memorable and also give my dad the travel that he had wished he could have done more of before he died. Jacqui had a good sense of humour, but I wasn't entirely sure she'd go for it. Perhaps if I told her that the DFAT regulations had all been complied with, she might just agree to it, though. Only thing I could do was ask. It was her after all, who had suggested I take Joel's head on holiday with me to Europe.

I rang her and asked what she thought. I could hear her tearing up over the phone. She thought it was a brilliant idea. So it was set. Finding something to put him in had taken some trial and error. There was a cat urn at one stage. (You read that right.) I went to a pet crematorium and told them I wanted a small, simple urn that would screw tight in my suitcase. I was a little wary of telling them exactly what I wanted it for, but I needn't have worried. Rather than the shock and possible disgust I was expecting (or laughter at least) I was met with a nonplussed response. "Oh we get lots of requests for that kind of thing. You'd be surprised," they said.

In the end I settled on the makeup jar though, as the urn was still far too big and much too heavy to fit inside my backpack. It was that, or the hair straightener had to go. Nope. And so the makeup jar was decided on; it's strange just how much makeup looks like human remains. Luckily, I'm neither overly sentimental nor religious. Or squeamish for that matter. Although I did need my husband to help me spoon the ashes out from the large urn he'd come home in – those things are not easy to get open! Using a dessert spoon to move parts of your father from a large plastic jar to a mineral makeup case is something everyone should try at least once in their lives.

I'm kidding of course. But we did laugh a lot at the ridiculousness of it all. Sometimes it's the only thing that can diffuse a situation that is just too awful to bear.

Waddling along towards the check-in desk at Cusco airport (waddle is all I could do under the weight of my pack and in the thin air at this altitude), I spotted an official-looking man setting up a trestle table. As I've mentioned, the customs officials right across South America had been wonderfully (if not worryingly) relaxed about bag-searching and screening throughout my whole trip, and now it appeared that my bag was going to be searched on this penultimate flight, before I even made it to the desk to pick up my ticket. This would have been no problem, I'd scattered Dad's ashes in all manner of places across the continent and I'd planned to be well and truly shot of them by now. However, abject terror spread through me slowly as I recalled …

Not three days before, I'd made the journey up to the ancient Incan ruins of Machu Picchu, along with Dad.

I hadn't had time to book the Inca trail, and so caught the train to Aguas Calientes and made the journey to the historical site on the next day, by bus. The ruins were as beautiful and mysterious as I'd hoped and I had a wonderful time poking around them with my tour-guided group (despite my usual distaste for tour-guided tours). But now I wanted to find a quiet spot to sit and say a last goodbye to Dad on my own. I had heard from one of the guides that we could walk up to the Sun Gate, which had unbelievable views across the whole of the ancient city. It wasn't as crowded up there, as it had to be climbed on foot and it was quite a slog. Not a long way – it was only about a two to three hour round trip. But being rather unfit, and at the altitude here in the highlands of Peru, I'd found it a real struggle. There were men and women twice, or maybe three times my age, trekking up there at what seemed like lightning speed. One Dutch couple was so lovely, as we continued to leap-frog each other, stopping at different intervals. Just as I'd overcome my heart palpitations and got my breath back after a break, I'd pass them having their own break and we'd each take a photo of the other at that spot. It was nice to have a little camaraderie up there, but I needed to find a place on my own to do the deed properly. I climbed ever higher and eventually found a rocky outcrop with an incredible vista which stretched out over Machu Picchu, now so far below me. I climbed out near the edge, nicely hidden behind some bushes and opened my day pack. I sat there looking over the ruins, and trying to find some way to make the connection between what I was seeing, and what I was there to do. It was not that Dad had wanted to come here himself, although he had wanted to travel more. He wasn't particularly fascinated by the Incas, though I'm sure he would have found them interesting.

I ruminated for a while, but in the end, I decided that I didn't need some deeper purpose or connection between this place and my dad. It was simply about bringing him along on this journey with me and paying homage to the fact that he would always be in my heart. I didn't need to scatter his ashes in a picturesque foreign place to discover that, but it would make a great Facebook photo. What I was really making for myself was a memory that would be forever special to me – because I'd taken him along to a place that I'd always wanted to see, and as I'd sat there marvelling at its beauty and history, I'd incorporated my memory of Dad. Now when I think about his death and how that time was in my life; I think of that mountain, the Sun Gate and sitting there in silence and reverence. It's a remarkable way to remember him.

I shook out what I could from the container, said a silent goodbye, and with a smile, I blew him away over the precipice and down towards the ruins of the city. As non-sentimental as I am, it still pleases me to know that there will always be a little piece of my dad in that place. His ashes would be carried by the wind, be rained upon and be soaked down into the earth. With every blade of grass or tree that grows in that spot, a little of him will grow with it. Over and over and over again.

Now standing at the pop-up customs line here in Cusco, my mind was far from that magical day, and instead buried in my backpack as I wondered whether or not that little container would be found. See, I still had the makeup jar in my backpack. I hadn't thrown it out. I hadn't disposed of the last of its contents: the chunky little bits of bone that wouldn't shake out through the dispenser. The customs officials … would they know what those little greyish-white fragments were? They looked like coral, or stones, or … well … bones. Crap! I needed to get rid of them. And quickly.

A plan formulated in my mind. Act cool. Do not race off and out of the line, as that will only make you look INCREDIBLY suspicious and make it very likely that you will be bowled over by airport security and locked in a dark cell. *Play it cool. Play it cool.*

I have always claimed not to have a poker face, and zero ability to appear calm when I'm screaming internally. But this could mean very dire circumstances and I needed to suck it up. Year 12 drama classes came back to me! I walked in what I hoped was a casual manner towards the customs official and smiled (what I hoped was) nonchalantly as I asked, 'Do you speak any English?'

"Yes," he replied, neither frightening nor friendly.

"See, I am really busting to use the bathroom and this looks like it might take a while," I gestured at the trestle table behind him. "Do you want to hold my bag while I go?" I beamed him a huge smile and held my backpack out towards him. Reverse psychology, you see. Heading off with your backpack to the toilets means drug dealer. Heading off to the bathroom while leaving your bag with an airport official means either (a) I'm busting, and you don't want me to wet myself while standing here on your clean, airport tiles or (b) there's a bomb in that damn bag and I'm going to detonate it as soon as I'm out of blast range!

Which scenario played out in his mind in those milliseconds, I'm not sure. But he quickly shook his head and pushed my bag back towards me.

"No, no! It's fine. You can take it with you!"

I swear I could have seen the tiniest bead of sweat form on his brow. I gratefully, although not too quickly, headed for the bathrooms. Being mindful not to walk too hastily, I stopped to ask another official where the ladies rooms were, and beamed him a great big *I'm just a girl who needs to pee, and I don't know where I am* smile. Within minutes I had my cubicle door locked and my backpack open on the toilet seat lid (hygiene be damned!), searching for that little container. Bingo. Right at the back of the pack, under my vacuum-seal clothes bags and hair straightener. Removing my backpack from the seat, now sans human remains receptacle, I sat down and tried desperately to get the lid off of the shake-out jar. It was useless. Without a pin or something to pull the lid off, I couldn't get out the chunky bits that were left inside. I struggled with it for an age. I was running out of time. There was nothing else for it, my plane was boarding soon and I needed to get through that damn inspection and get my ticket. I did something that I've never done before. I don't know what came over me. I am an Atheist and a sceptic. I don't believe in an afterlife, I don't believe in ghosts, I have no spiritual inclinations whatsoever. But he was still my dad, and while he may no longer have been around to hear me, I still afforded him a great deal of respect. And so, I sat down and I had a chat with him. Well, with what remained of him.

"Dad," I said, in inner monologue (lest raise suspicion from surrounding toilet-goers), "It's been a great trip, and don't think I've forgotten that you've been tucked in there with me all the way. But this is the end of the line for you. Thanks for the thrills. I love you."

With that, I opened the slot for the sanitary bin in the third cubicle at the north-end toilets of Cusco International Airport and slid what was left of Dad inside. I like to think those were bits he wasn't overly fond of. Perhaps his toe nails and his left pinky, maybe his elbow. I also like to think he would have had a huge laugh about it. He most definitely would have smacked me up the side of the head gently, and told me that I was a bloody idiot for the whole harebrained scheme.

I left those bathrooms a fraction lighter, and without a fear of instant incarceration, and headed for the check-in line, bound for Buenos Aires and then – home.

15

Lavers Hill
(Great Ocean Walk, Australia)

March, 2015 – I was still on this Godforsaken hike in Victoria. I'd gotten my life-(and feet) saving lift to Johanna Beach after meeting Geraldine and Phil at the Aire River campsite.

After saying goodbye to my saviours and their gleaming white (A-van) chariot, I sat down with the rest of Tony and Lisa's hiking group that had since shown up. Bec hadn't arrived yet, but I was sure she'd be along soon. As I still had no phone signal and Joel hadn't heard from me for a couple of days now, I borrowed a phone from one of the group and made a quick call to let him know that I was alive and that I would be on my way to Laver's Hill tomorrow. He was definitely relieved to hear that I'd be heading back to civilisation, and tried to assure me that it was the best decision given the circumstances. I appreciated his support but I couldn't help feeling like I'd let myself down. I felt like a lump of useless flubber, really. Not fit enough for this hike. Not fit enough for much. A let-down who would always be just a little bit fat and a little bit average.

I handed the phone back to the man I'd borrowed it from and thanked him again, then sat down just outside of the group. They'd spread out across the low table and proceeded to assess their gear and their feet as they waited for Abby (the shuttle bus operator) to arrive with their ride back to Apollo Bay. As had happened so many times already on this trip, and on many of my travels in fact, I began to feel unworthy; like a burden and an outsider. Self-doubt crept in like an old and unwelcome acquaintance who I can never seem to avoid. Outwardly, I was calm and collected and nonchalant about being alone and defeated. Inside, I wanted to cry. And not for the first time, I wanted to be back at home with Joel – warm and in my own lounge room. I wanted to be curled up on the couch with a cup of tea and a movie, with the elements shut out by the warm cocoon of my windows. I wanted to feel safe and worthy and … wanted.

While I sat and tried to look small and non-burdensome, Tony and Lisa made small talk. They assured me that it had happened to everyone; blisters getting the better of each of them at some stage. Their words did make me feel a little better, although I did feel a tiny suspicion that they were just saying that to make me feel less awkward. Thankfully I didn't have to sit there too long before Bec showed up. She was bouncing along as usual, and beaming as she arrived at the group and they congratulated her on her arrival. Shortly after, Abby and his rescue van showed up.

Still extremely sore and with my feet protesting, I hobbled over towards the van. As each of the group threw their backpacks into the trailer and hopped into the van, Abby took no notice of Bec and I whatsoever. I realised he thought that we were with the group heading out now, and I was more than a little tempted to just throw my pack in and go with them. Alas, we stood there patiently and waited for him to finish with everyone else's gear. When he was finally ready to jump into the driver's seat, he turned around and looked shocked at the two of us still standing there.

"Hi!" I chirped, with more confidence than I felt. "We are not with the group. We're actually hoping that you might be able to give us a lift to Lavers Hill tomorrow morning if you're not too busy?"

He scratched his chin and pulled out a large black diary from inside the van. As he opened it to the correct day and pondered his handwritten schedule I continued.

"See, my feet are shot. Bec wants to continue on, but we're hoping to take a day off tomorrow, stay in Lavers Hill and then Bec wants to be dropped back onto the trail at Ryan's Den the next day while I camp at Devil's Kitchen and wait for her."

He gave me a puzzled look, asked me to repeat and then shook his head. I panicked a little.

"Don't worry, we'll sort you out. Let's just get you to Lavers Hill tomorrow and then you can call me from there tomorrow night after you've had a meal at the pub and a warm shower."

He had me at the words 'pub' and 'shower'. Relief once again washed over me. This was a man who had it handled. He wasn't going to leave us stranded, and he was a can-do kind of guy. I asked him how much we'd owe him, knowing that the trip back from the end of the hike to Apollo Bay was going to cost us $90. I was expecting it to be quite a bit, with all of the drop offs and pickups we'd need over the next few days.

"We'll work it out later. I'll see you in the morning. 8:00 am, right here." He pointed to the spot where we stood. "Campsite's up that hill, when you go through the gate and get to the tyre-tracks, take that route; it's the new path they're putting in."

I didn't know whether to be relived at the ease of his manner or to be wary at how much I was going to be out of pocket. I didn't much care at this point, as I didn't really have another option. With that, he was in his van and off he went, taking Tony, Lisa and crew with him. Bec and I waved them goodbye and picked up our packs once more.

I explained to Bec the drama we'd had in trying to find the campsite (if you remember, Phil was trundling up and down tracks and trying to find it, to no avail). But Abby's advice at least put our minds at ease that it was in fact up the hill where we had supposed it was meant to be. Bec and I trudged up the hill and I had new vigour now that I knew that I had safely secured a ride for tomorrow and that my feet would continue to get a break. I was more than a little chuffed at the idea of a soft bed, a shower and a beer the next night. Not to mention a pub meal.

We wandered up the hill and took a couple of false turns before we finally found the campsite. Atop a cliff, it overlooked Johanna Beach below and we watched warily as a storm rolled in. We set up camp with the most incredible views over the coastline and out to the horizon. It was already blisteringly cold and the sun hadn't yet set. The wind was picking up and we could see the dark clouds looming ever closer. After several discussions, we decided that we'd best move into the bush behind the shelter building, as we'd have a pretty uncomfortable night ahead of us if the wind got any worse. We picked our tents up whole, without dismantling them, and carried them like blow-up castles back into the bush behind us. We picked what we assessed as the least-windy patch of dirt and reset our camp. That night as the wind howled we sat inside the shelter and watched the setting sun splash colours across the darkening sky. Our clifftop camp was surely one of the most incredible vantage points I've ever had for watching the sun set over the Australian sky.

That night, as we curled up inside our tents and tried to keep warm, it occurred to me how utterly alone and vulnerable we were out there. The landscape back there, tucked away in the bush reminded me eerily of prime hunting grounds for Ivan Milat types (an Australian serial killer, for those non-Aussies). I slept fitfully, with my pocket knife hugged closely to my side and stared out into the darkness until the sun finally began to rise.

When it was at last light enough to get up and use the 'bathroom' (read: patch of grass and biodegradable toilet paper) without fear of being murdered by serial killers or dangerous wildlife, I peeled myself from my sleeping bag and extricated myself from my tent with considerable difficulty. I was still very sore and stiff. I sure was looking forward to my first shower that week. Bec soon rose and we packed up camp after our usual breakfasts and a cup of tea each. It was still freezing cold, as it was not yet 7:00 am. We figured that with the kind of shape my feet were still in, we should give ourselves the best part of an hour to make it back down the hill and to the pickup spot. Luckily we did, as I actually skipped quite quickly down the hill, but Bec somehow took a different route and got a little lost. I was shocked to arrive before she did, and saw Abby's van in the distance, having passed the camp without stopping. I ran, in my mangled, demented way, and called out after him. As I reached the pickup spot, I saw Bec emerge from the long grass and Abby, thankfully, pull back around after doing a lap of the carpark. It was only quarter to eight and he was early. Bec made it down to the van, and we eagerly chucked our bags in towards the empty seats before hopping in ourselves and getting comfortable. The driver today was not Abby, as it turned out. In my haste I hadn't noticed, but we had a much older gentleman who told us his name was Peter.

Peter was friendly and cheerful, and thanked us for being on time (I got this sense from his tone that he was used to hikers and campers showing up late), and we in turn thanked him for not driving off without us. He assured us that he was just doing laps to make sure we weren't waiting at one of the several other benches dotted around the large carpark. With that, we were off to Lavers Hill.

Peter asked us where we were staying and we told him we'd been advised to stay at 'the Pub'. We didn't exactly know what that meant, but assumed it would be the only pub in town, or else we'd have been given more instructions from Tony and Abby. Yes, Peter confirmed, we should stay at 'the pub'.

"Just don't stay at that new joint across the road from the store," he advised us, with an ominous and dark tone to his voice. Until then he'd been jovial and upbeat, so I wasn't quite sure what had brought that tone on. I was curious.

"What do you mean, Peter? Is it a bit dodgy or something?" I asked.

"I think you heard me right, eh? Just don't stay there and that's all I'm gonna say!" He gave me a frown through the rear vision mirror and I could tell that he would say no more on the subject. I was truly intrigued now, if not a little suspicious that perhaps Peter and 'the other place' had some ancient family feud going on!

"I'll drop you girls off at the store, which will be open now, and you can get yourself something to eat and drink before you go down to the pub later," he explained. That sounded like a fair plan to me, and we sat contentedly chatting away for the half-hour ride out of Johanna Beach.

True to his word, Peter pulled up outside the 'store' which was also the petrol station and somewhat of a roadhouse café. The 'other place' stood in clear view of the store, sitting across the road and actually, I thought at least, looked rather inviting. It was built in the large Queenslander style, with a huge balcony that circled the entire property, and signs boasting 'best steak in town' and 'open breakfast, lunch and dinner!'

Peter bade us a warm goodbye and refused to take any cash from me, saying simply 'sort it out with Abby when you speak to him.' And then, he was off, waving and giving us a big smile as he left. We picked up our packs and headed inside to our first taste of civilisation since we'd left to start the hike from Apollo Bay. There was a friendly old guy behind the counter who told us to take a seat over in the large dining area and that he'd be over in a second. I could see him setting up a few things, as they'd obviously not been open long yet that morning, and soon he headed over to ask us what we'd like. I asked for a coffee while Bec settled on a hot chocolate after I gave her the '*don't you DARE order nothing*' face. She really was a strange creature and I couldn't wrap my head around why she never wanted to eat or drink at opportunities like this. I also ordered a chunky steak pie. It's not that I was overly hungry, as we'd had breakfast only a couple of hours ago, but I was just glad to be inside and warm and actually have *options* like pies and coffees and the like.

As we sat and drank, and as I munched away on my pie (it was delicious, by the way), we were entertained outside by a group of red parrots who fluttered from the lush green garden to the handmade bird-feeders dotted beneath the trees. There was obviously a bird lover among us here somewhere. I went over to question the store owner about when we should expect the pub to be open and in which direction we should head.

I added, "Oh, and we were told not to stay in the place across the road?"

"Oh no!" he said, as he shook his head. "Peter's right, don't stay there!"

Again, I was intrigued. "Why?" I asked, "Is it a bit crap? Is it dodgy?"

He didn't answer, but nodded in that *you-know-what-I-mean* kind of way, and then looked up and pointed out the door. (I hate to disappoint you, reader, but we never did find out what was so wrong about that 'other place'. Mystery unsolved, I'm afraid.)

"Here's Geoff now. He owns the pub; have a chat to him when he comes inside!" as though this were a morning ritual, and there was nothing serendipitous about it. He chuckled and greeted Geoff as he strolled through the door.

"Geoff, these young ladies want a room for tonight."

Geoff looked around to see me standing next to the magazines and Bec sitting over by the windows, still sipping slowly at her hot chocolate. I hoped we didn't look too feral, but there was no mistaking that the store owner was talking about us; there was no one else in the place yet.

Casually, he smiled, picked up and paid for a paper and said, "Oh yeah, we've got some rooms free tonight. Come on down and see me when you're finished and I'll sort you out."

He had an easy, old-school way about him and he instantly reminded me of my dad. Rough around the edges and unshaven, his scruffy hair sat in that unkempt-yet-charming way that Dad's had. He had more than a little grey running through his beard and dirt under his fingernails suggesting he worked hard at something greasy. Dad's nails were almost permanently grease-stained, and I have always associated that trait with hard work and competence in *that I-can-fix-anything-with-enough-super-glue-and-nails* kind of way that some older men have.

"What time do you open?" I asked

"Oh just come down whenever you're ready," he said. "I'll be there." With that, he smiled and left the store. When we'd finished our drinks and I'd passed back my plate to the lady now manning the counter, we said our thanks to the store owner and headed out into the cold again. We headed down the road, shoulders bowed against the wind, in the direction we'd been told. It was nice to be in a town again, passing little houses and cottages and even the odd garbage bin. I just hoped we didn't look homeless … or smell bad enough to attract stray dogs … or vultures.

Soon enough, we crested a hill and could make out a sign for the pub. There was also a store, a gas pump, a parking lot of caravans and a demountable building which appeared to house three separate motel rooms. Unsure of where exactly we'd find Geoff, we opted to try the first door – the pub door.

It creaked, heavy on its hinges, as I pushed it open and the smell of a log fire hit my nostrils.

"Hello?" I uttered, in a hopeful tone.

"Come on in," answered Geoff, and sure enough as I rounded a second doorway into the pub proper, there he was, sitting at a table in front of an open log fire, reading the paper he'd just bought at the shop.

"So, I've got a couple of rooms you can try. They're a bit overpriced. You see, I don't own the rooms. I just look after them. I'll give you the key to room number one, you come back and tell me if you don't like it, ok?" He fetched a key and leather keychain from behind the bar and handed it to us, then showed us outside and pointed to the demountable building.

"Don't worry, Geoff. If it's got a bed, and a shower and a heater, we'll be happy," I told him.

He smiled and looked encouraged by that, and headed back to his fire while we made for the room. Fitting the key into the lock, I had to jiggle it a bit before it opened and we made our way inside. The room was simply furnished with queen bed, single bedside table and TV unit. Behind the bedroom was a door to the small ensuite. There were no such extravagances as little hotel shampoos and conditioners but there were two towels, face towels and soap; and that was all we needed. I took dibs on first shower, as Bec wasn't fazed. I used my soap to also wash my spare tights, every pair of underwear that I wasn't wearing, and my long-sleeve top. I stood under that blissfully hot water and washed my hair, watching the dirty water pool on the tiles before being sucked down the drain and out of my life. I washed and cleaned my blistered and battered feet and even they felt better just for having being given a thorough cleaning. I felt a million bucks when I finally came out, skin steaming and mirror fogged from the heat.

"Your turn," I uttered, serenely, as I hung my wet things out on the radiator and climbed into the bed and under the soft, gorgeous covers. It was still really early, but thankfully in a one-horse town like Lavers Hill there seemed to be no such thing as a 2:00 pm check-in. By 11:00 am we were both showered, shaved and ready for a nap in the gloriously HUGE queen bed. At home I sleep on a king-sized bed; however, after a few days in the confines of my one-man ultralight tent and two-third length sleeping mat, this bed felt genuinely enormous. The novelty of having the TV on in the background also wasn't lost on me, and I drifted off to sleep as though I were floating on a cloud of pure bliss.

16

GOW is Finally Over

After our gorgeous nap, we waited for our freshly washed (in the shower) clothes to dry on the radiator and busied ourselves unpacking our now completely disorganised backpacks. I took delight, as I always do, in sorting my things into piles such as 'you need that near the top', 'this is somewhat important but not needed in an emergency' and 'this is useless, you may now throw it away'. Relieving my pack of all the now-unnecessary items was like a guilty pleasure and gave me some small sense of control, worthiness and capableness.

Once I'd successfully repacked the 'necessary' piles back neatly into my bag, I was delighted to feel it now considerably lighter as I lifted it. Bec and I then dressed in our almost-dry clothes and brushed our freshly washed hair (I would have killed for a blow dryer and straightener at this point, but beggars can't be choosers, as they say.) We headed out from our little room through the chilly late afternoon air and towards the pub, in search of a hot meal and a cold beer. Bristling and rubbing our hands, we pushed through the saloon-style doors and into the glorious warmth of the tavern. Geoff was nowhere to be seen, but behind the counter stood a young blonde woman who smiled warmly as we approached. Seeing as we were perhaps the only people staying there that night, she was probably briefed earlier on the two scruffy hikers that she could expect to see, and I felt no need to explain who we were as we greedily perused the beers and ciders on offer.

"You girls after some dinner as well?" she asked. Well, it was more of a statement than a question, as she looked knowingly at us and we gave her simply enthusiastic nods in return. It was all I could do to not drool all over the bar top, at this stage. She handed over our drinks (a pint of cider for each of us) and sat us down with a couple of menus. To Bec's delight, chicken parmigiana featured on the menu and to my glee – so did a chicken curry. I can never go past a curry and rice, and pub curries are always some of the best (who wouldv'e thought?)

Kelly (for that was her name) came over to have a chat with us and ask us about our hike. Turns out she had indeed been briefed on our escapades, and was quite interested in how far we'd come. Like world-weary sailors, we regaled her with tales of struggle, torment and those infernal blisters! She seemed suitably impressed by our efforts, mine included, despite my obvious inferior abilities. The warm food, huge cider and conversation with Kelly gave me another much-needed boost and it felt great to be on the other side of some of those stories, now able to tell them rather than live them. I really had no desire to get back out there onto the cold and gruelling track and I justified this to myself by calculating the number of crazy stories I'd collected, and evaluating the journey on this currency alone. Scars? Check! Near-death experiences? Sure! Colourful characters? Yes! Surely the trip had served its purpose of adventure and achievement? Another cider, I decided, and I'd think about it later. For now, I just wanted to enjoy this night.

Well-fed and after a few more drinks, we decided to play some pool. I am terrible, really, really terrible at pool. My whole family are certified pool-sharks, and I somehow missed that gene entirely. But the occasion called for some kind of activity to prolong our merry night in the small pub in the middle of nowhere, and so, we played. The bar was starting to fill up a little now, with regulars piling in and being greeted like old friends. We even caught a glimpse of Geoff every now and again as he shuffled between the kitchen and the front of house, delivering meals to hungry diners.

While Bec had assured me that she too was rubbish at pool, I hadn't believed her for a second and expected to have my ass thoroughly handed to me over the table. Turns out she wasn't lying, and we knocked the balls around at a fairly even rate, keeping the game going for a respectable amount of time. Just about the only 'respectable' aspect of our game, as it turned out. A great battle ensued, as we fought equally miserably at nudging our colours around the table (there's probably a technical term for a pool table, like a 'green' or something … but I'm yet to hear it) for near an hour. While we were duelling, a couple had entered the salon and sat themselves nearby. Clearly waiting for drinks and perhaps some takeaway food, they amused themselves by scoffing at our efforts. Quite merry on cider and high on the warmth of the evening inside the pub, I called over to them,

"You think we're doing this on purpose? We're not. We are really, truly, this bad!"

The gent of the pair replied quickly, laughing, "I thought you must be putting it on! We can't believe you're both so terrible!"

We all fell around laughing, and as Bec and I finally finished the game (I won! Huzzah! Some dignity returned to my humble self-deprecating self) we went over to chat with the couple. They were visiting from the UK, and were waiting for some hot chips to take on their car trip down to the nearby glow-worm caves. We all ordered more drinks and while we sat around waiting for their hot chips, Rob and Alice filled us in on their travels.

Alice had been to Australia once before, to visit a friend, however this was Rob's first trip abroad. We were equally as curious to find out how they'd ended up here as they were about us. Turns out that on her last trip, Alice had heard about the nearby glow-worm caves and was keen to visit them now that she was back again. Rob raised his eyebrows as she was explaining this, and I got the impression that perhaps this wasn't first on his list of 'fun things to do when you're in Australia where just about everything wants to kill you before breakfast'. I caught his eye and gave him a sympathetic wink and a chuckle. After all, no one understood better than me what it was like to be afraid of … anything.

When their chips finally arrived and we'd all had a good laugh getting to know about each other, Alice asked tentatively if we'd like to come along to the glow-worm cave. Without hesitation we agreed, and I saw the relief instantly in Rob's face. Having a couple of Aussies around would surely reduce their chances of meeting a John Jarret-esque killer in the dark?

We bundled up into their car and headed in the general direction (Alice's recollection was vague) of the glow-worms. Sure enough, there were handy tourist signs to guide us from the highway and down a muddy track to the carpark. There were no other cars around, and it was a black night. I shivered, and Rob offered me his jacket (this cold was nothing to a couple of Brits!). We all set off down the track, with nothing but our smartphones to guide us through the dimness. While Rob fretted about murderers and large things that might kill him, I was more concerned about leeches. Ugh!

We'd been lucky enough to entirely avoid leeches on our hike so far, as the scrub had been far too dry to support their tedious existence. (Although, I'm sure they were there somewhere, just waiting for rain and a fleshy ankle to sink their fangs into!) But here on the glow-worm track, the ground was sodden and leafy; perfect leech territory. I had only my runners on, and no socks. Perfect leech invitation: juicy, bare ankles. Bleargh! I shuddered at the thought and warned the others to keep an eye out. Rob was still no more fazed about the leeches, as he worried about other imaginary maladies.

I had good reason to be fearful of leeches. While training for the GOW, Joel and I had hiked through the Sunshine Coast hinterland one weekend. Despite the dry conditions, it turned out that the Sunshine Coast was prime leechy habitat. We were totally unprepared. I had on my usual runners and above-ankle leggings garb – and not for the first time, my juicy, bare ankles were exposed. (When would I ever learn?) I found myself obsessively checking for leeches every few feet – and for good reason! I pulled off no less than a dozen leeches throughout that 16-plus kilometre hike. I was so preoccupied with it that I started imagining that every brush against my ankles was another leech. More often than not, it was. They were everywhere; the little blood suckers! I managed to flick off each one with a squeal, well before they'd been able to grab hold. Obsessiveness wins! Joel laughed at me and made jokes about my squeamishness. In actual fact, it was not the blood-sucking that bothered me, but more so the difficulty in getting them off and the risk of infection should I pull one off with force. Much to his chagrin and my eternal amusement, we had barely stopped at the rest spot for a breather before I noticed a HUGE brown attachment to Joel's ankle. LEECH! I pointed it out to him (calmly) and he jumped, before grabbing a stick and flicking it away. The thing had gorged itself fat on his ankle and simply toppled to the ground – blood drunk. Joel did his best not to look disgusted (lest I hold it over his head forever) and tried to calm himself. His ankle bled profusely and I got to practise my bandaging skills (luckily I'd brought the first aid kit!)

Back at the glow-worm track, we trudged and trudged, made wrong turns and lost our way, despite the clearly marked track. It was dark, after all, and we were searching via phone-light. While I regularly checked my ankles, the others plugged on ahead and I was left to bring up the rear (and no doubt, deal with any murderers that chose the age-old *sneak-up-behind* technique.) Against all scary odds, finally a gasp came from the front of the queue. Bec had located something sparkly on the rock wall.

Swinging our phone-lights upwards as we stood on a small wooden bridge, we saw a rocky cliff hung heavy with moss and ferns and … glow-worms! Squillions of them! Switching off all of our lights made it much easier to see; they were everywhere. It was like a giant string of fairy lights had been stretched across every inch of the wall. They glittered and sparkled and danced. We all discussed the evolutionary advantages of worms with glowing butts and decided that it must have something to do with mating and being the worm with the prettiest, sparkly-est bottom. The sparkling worm gets the … worm booty? In the cold and dark, as we all huddled around and kept an ear out for baddies, it occurred to me what an odd thing it was that I was here at the southern tip of Australia with a couple of Brits and a mate, after a huge hike (that wasn't over yet), staring at luminescent insects and discussing their mating habits. It was one of my favourite moments of the trip. None of us bothered to highlight the fact that we hadn't actually made it to the 'caves' yet. The sparkly wall hosted enough glow-worm activity for us, thanks! Let's get out of the dark before we tempt fate, and murderous locals!

Rob and Alice dropped us back at our room at the pub, once we'd all had our fill of wormy glow. We thanked them for the ride, they thanked us for the Aussie protection (ha!) and they were off in to the night.

We'd decided to stay another night at Laver's Hill and discuss our options. We still hadn't paid the shuttle driver and when I'd tried he waved us away with a hand and said, 'I'll call ya tomorrow at the pub and we'll sort you out then.' Country hospitality! The next night, as we ate another amazing home cooked meal in the pub, Kelly came out baring a cordless phone.

"It's for you, it's Abby."

Several other patrons looked around in awe as if to say, 'They get their phone calls here? How well connected are these girls?' They clearly weren't familiar with the GOW shuttle's relaxed operations. I basked in the tiny amount of fame that it seemed to afford us, and took the call while shovelling a chip into my face.

"G'day Abby! What's up?"

"You girls want to get back on to the track at Devil's Kitchen. Ryan's Den campsite is too far from the road and we can't drop you close enough; you'll never make it with the state of your feet. Now mind you, the walk from the carpark to Devil's Kitchen is still a couple of kilometres. Do you think you can manage that? I will pick you up in the morning, and Bec can carry on to the Twelve Apostles and the finish line. We'll pick her up from there and shoot you back to Apollo Bay. How's that sound?"

I asked for a few minutes to relay that back to Bec and clear with her. Abby agreed to give us a call back in a little while, at the bar. We perused our map and discovered that it was indeed quite a hike into Ryan's Den. Bec wasn't keen for hiking that far, and then further to Devil's Kitchen on her own as the weather had turned, and the terrain was much rougher still. We agreed that we'd get dropped off at Devil's Kitchen the next morning, we'd hike in, stay the night and she'd set off the next day on the final leg to the Twelve Apostles while I hiked back out to my lift – just as Abby had suggested.

And so, the next day we were off bright and early at 8:00 am. The hike from the carpark at the peak of Devil's Kitchen was a nightmare. 'Only a couple of kilometres' turned out to be more like 6 to 8 ks by our calculations, as we came across miles and miles of one of my least favourite things in the world: switchbacks. Sure, they're designed to reduce the steep grade with which you ascend and descend a mountain, but they have the infuriating effect of tripling the distance you have to walk. I'd rather have just slid down the damn hill, and might have considered it, if it weren't for the steep rocky cliffs that dotted the hillside. It took us hours. My feet and groin injuries suffered immensely. Once again, I wanted to lie down and die. And still, not for the last time, Bec was exceedingly patient and helpful as she always is. I was a grumbly, whingey, hot mess, as I always am.

Finally, mercifully, we made it to camp. The one consolation to that nightmare hike was the 'Loo with a View' which we'd read about it our guidebook. It really was spectacular (if you don't mind the spiders; which of course, I do). Climb to the top of a wooden staircase to a raised outhouse and you can sit and make your ablutions with a view across the rolling hills and out to the Tasman. It's pretty incredible. I tried to appreciate it fully, while simultaneously ignoring the large cobwebs that hung about. I was too tired to do the spider dance with any curious arachnids. Kill me if you will, but do it quickly, I thought.

We spent the rest of the day admiring the view from a bench near our campsite (despite the freezing temperatures) and eating the rest of Bec's instant mashed potato. Yum! We drank many a cup of tea and regaled each other with stories of our adventure so far. Only one more day to go: a 16k hike in rough terrain for Bec and a 6–8k hike back to the carpark for me. I slept fitfully in the cold that night and arose to the sound of Bec up early and packing her gear.

Now that we were light on food, each of our packs was lighter and emptier. I took as much of Bec's gear as I could fit, in order to make her last stretch a little easier. I had a difficult hike ahead of me, with my shredded feet and still-injured groin, but I felt guilt at leaving Bec to do so much of this hike alone. She set off after packing up, and I had a couple of hours to while away, drinking tea and slowly getting my gear together. Finally, I headed out of camp and made my way back through the infuriating switchbacks and scrub lands. It was horrible. Every time I crested a hill and was sure I must be about to break through the trees and stumble onto the carpark, the track would take another turn that I didn't remember, and present to me yet another hill to climb and another set of switchbacks to battle. Fucking switchbacks, I thought. If I never see another Goddamn switchback again in my life, it will be too Goddamn soon! I grumbled and swore my way through the kilometres. I cried a little. It rained. I put my raincoat on. I got too hot and took it off again. I got soaked. I sweated. My feet hurt. My groin hurt. My legs hurt. My feet hurt more. I tripped over in the mud and came crashing down on my ass. I laughed at the sheer ridiculousness of myself, while nobody was around to see it. I must look a treat, I thought!

Finally, finally, finally, I saw a car. Nope. One carpark too soon. Rogue carpark. But I was close. I could see the tip of the outlook, and that meant; the pickup spot. When I burst through the last of the trees at last, it was rather anticlimactic. There was no one around. There were no shelters or benches to sit at. There was only a sign, showing a map to the lookout (fuck that, I've seen enough of this place!) and a few warnings about leeches and mosquitoes. None of which had been a problem, thank goodness! I had nothing to do but sit and wait for my ride. I was two hours early. Despite my difficulties in making that last leg back, I was nothing if not punctual.

The wind blew a gale, and I shivered uncontrollably as it then started to rain almost horizontally. The back of my legs were soaking wet, as I stood on the less-windy side of the sign. I MacGyver'd a lean-to shelter with my ground tarp and a few occy-straps against the legs of the signage. It made a hell of a racket, as the wind bashed against it, but it kept me dry and a little warmer. There I sat, waiting for the pickup shuttle to arrive. He was late, and I was starting to worry that he'd forgotten me. Panic and bile rose in my throat as the minutes ticked by. I had no mobile coverage and couldn't make a call. A couple of cars swung through, on their way to check out the lookout. Each of them asked if I needed a ride, and I thanked them for their offers (and their bravery, as I must have looked like a mad person up there, huddled against my big blue tarp and shivering myself silly), but regretfully declined. I had to wait it out and hope that my ride would arrive.

And of course, he eventually did. Like a knight in shining white minivan, Abby's elderly driver bundled out of the bus and helped me with my pack; but not before congratulating me on my makeshift shelter; he was genuinely impressed. Maybe I wasn't so useless after all, hey? With his sincere apologies for being late and my 'don't even worry about it' we were on our way to pick up Bec at the Twelve Apostles and then – back to Apollo Bay and civilisation.

We drove past the famous Apostles, and I barely registered the gravitas that they deserved. Bec was already waiting for us, and looked almost as cold as I had until the shuttle's heating had kicked in and thawed me out. I opened the door before the driver could even make his way around to the passenger side. 'Get in, get in, it's warm!' I beamed. We embraced as she bundled in to the van, and we grinned at each other. Like a couple of war veterans, or crazy adventurers, muddy, stinky and worse for wear; we felt as though we'd done something incredible. I was so proud of Bec. I was proud of me, too – despite my not being able to make it all the way on foot. We'd really done something adventurous; we'd done something out of our comfort zone; something brave; something different; something *other*.

We'd survived.

17

A Note on Travel

ow, sitting at my desk and putting these words to paper (or computer), I am not holed up in a sub-par hostel. I'm not sitting atop a rickety bed, looking out across a northern-hemispherical sunset. I am sitting at home, surrounded by piles of paper and lists of tasks for work on Monday. Among my printer and staplers and highlighters and pens are little stashes of foreign currency that I never managed to spend; a reminder of my times in faraway places. Like postcards to myself, I stumble across an Argentinian *diez pesos* note when I'm looking for a paperclip. I smile. I stash it back in its spot. I find the paperclip.

This book has been a labour of love. But a labour of *weekend* love. Slogging it out at work, we plug away the hours and tally up the years. Now well and truly out of my 20s, those interminable questions niggle at me. When will we buy a home? When will we start properly saving (and stop pissing our money up against the proverbial wall)? Enough dinners out, enough espresso martinis! When will we have kids? When will we invest? What about Intel? What about wind farming? When should we get a bigger TV? When will I get a promotion? When, what, when, when?

I don't tend to dwell on regrets; it's not my style. I know that each and every choice I've made in my life has led me to where I am now – and that is something to be grateful for. But the older I get, the more I slog away working for somebody else, the more often I get pangs of dread. Like a red hot poker in the eye, I'm suddenly overcome with a genuinely physical reaction. The veins and tendons in my hands will ache, as they do when I am trying not to cry. My throat will constrict. My stomach will drop. My head will swim. I recognise this reaction, as it's the same one I've felt many times; when the loss of my dad will wash over me like a big, crushing wave from nowhere. I diagnose it as panic immediately.

If anything, we're late bloomers, my husband and I. Soon it will be soccer practice, five serves of veggies a day, school fees, home insurance, maternity leave, corporate ladder climbing and annual trips to the snow. If we're lucky. I can't ski. I'll be waiting in the bar.

And don't get me wrong, family and career and owning a home are all admirable pursuits. But what about now? What about adventure and drab hostels and questionable roadside curries? What about bumpy bus rides to the middle of nowhere? What about dodgy cab drivers and struggling with translation and the pure exhaustion of having spent hours and days on the road? What about marvelling at a truly indescribable scene on the other side of the world; a sunrise, a temple, a herd of cattle crossing the dirt strip which barely passes for a road? What about grimy clothes and well-worn backpacks? What about crazy ideas and being ill-equipped and under-prepared? Didn't Elizabeth Gilbert teach us anything?

As much as I've grumbled about dodgy Bolivians, piss-weak showers, indecipherable accents, lumpy beds and all of the myriad maladies associated with travel, I simply love the *otherness* of it all. I crave it daily, and I look back on it fondly.

You only have to check your Facebook feed to find the latest inspirational quote set against a backdrop of a mysterious mountain peak, *'Do what you love, and the money will follow'*. Every man's dog is an expert. I blame you, Elizabeth!

Leap and the net will appear. Life's too short. *C'est la vie. Carpe Diem*. Life is what happens when you're busy making plans. Two shakes of a monkey's uncle. (What? Ok, so maybe not that one!)

Far be it for me to give advice. For who am I to give it? Certainly no expert on life or travel. On anything, for that matter. After all, this isn't a self-help book. But for what it's worth, here's my two pesos (and that might not be much, I concede): take any old adage. They're cliché's for a reason, after all. What do you love? Just do it. Plans can wait. The world is out there. You simply need to go and find it. Go and find your *otherness*. You'll never forgive yourself if you don't.

* * * *

… and if one day you find yourself stranded in Djibouti, with a flat tyre and a rapidly depleting water supply? My lawyers assure me that I hold no legal responsibility for your situation.

But if you're sitting on the side of the road there, waiting for a gang of friendly locals to come and help you with the spare, and you're grinning to yourself that 'yes, this is what life is about', then I'll take full credit. You're welcome! You can thank me via my website. Or maybe we'll meet on the road one day, and you can tell me all about it.

About the Author

Maggie Harris is an Australian girl, born and raised in suburbia. She currently lives on the Gold Coast in Queensland and spends her days drinking tea and dreaming, and just generally wishing she was elsewhere. An Atheist, a left-wing libertarian and staunch LGBTI equal rights supporter, Maggie studies religion (at times) and pays student loans on degrees she never finished.

While her day job pays the bills, it's really not anything to write home about. So, she travels when she can. The problem is, she hates to plan. She tends to jump on a plane to 'see what happens' at the other end.

Otherness is a collection of tales from Maggie's travels. Some of these tales are delightful. Some are sad. Some are hilarious (she thinks). Many of them involve a great deal of stupidity. She hopes it makes for interesting reading, at least. If nothing else, she can laugh in hindsight at all of her escapades.

Being less than prepared hasn't killed her yet. But give it time.

May her headstone read:

'Well, that was interesting …'

Printed in Great Britain
by Amazon